User's Guide

User's Guide

To Accompany the 11th Edition of Intellectual Disability: Definition, Classification, and Systems of Supports

Applications for Clinicians, Educators, Organizations Providing Supports, Policymakers, Family Members and Advocates, and Health Care Professionsals

Developed by the AAIDD User's Guide Work Group

Robert L. Schalock, Ruth Luckasson, Val Bradley, Wil Buntinx, Yves Lachapelle, Karrie A. Shogren, Martha E. Snell, James R. Thompson, Marc Tassé, Miguel A. Verdugo-Alonso, and Michael L. Wehmeyer

American Association on Intellectual and Developmental Disabilities

© 2012 by American Association on Intellectual and Developmental Disabilities

All rights reserved. No part of this book may be reproduced or transmitted in any form or by any means, electronic or mechanical, including photocopying, recording, or by any information storage and retrieval system, without permission in writing from the publisher.

Printed in the United States of America

Contents

Overview and Purpose of the User's Guide vii

List of Tables ix

List of Figures x

Chapter 1   Overview of the 2010 AAIDD Definition, Classification, and Systems of Supports 1

Chapter 2   Relevance of the 2010 AAIDD System to Professionalism and Professional Responsibilities 7

Chapter 3   Applications for Clinicians in the Diagnosis of Intellectual Disability 13

Chapter 4   Applications for Educators 29

Chapter 5   Applications for Organizations Providing Supports 41

Chapter 6   Applications for Policymakers 49

Chapter 7   Applications for Family Members and Advocates 59

Chapter 8   Applications for Health Care Professionals 63

Glossary 69

References 77

Subject Index 83

OVERVIEW

PURPOSE OF THE USER'S GUIDE

Professionals in the field of intellectual disability (ID) are responsible for making decisions and recommendations regarding the diagnosis, classification, and planning of individualized supports for persons with ID. These decisions need to be based on best practices in ID, professional standards, professional ethics, and clinical judgment. These four professional responsibility requirements are used to try to make excellent decisions or recommendations, and ultimately to help improve the welfare and personal well-being of people with ID. Essential to those efforts is a clear understanding of ID and best practices regarding the diagnosis, classification, and planning of individualized supports for persons with ID. The primary purpose of this *User's Guide* is to provide that clear understanding of ID and summarize best practices in the field. Its authors are a subgroup of the AAIDD 2010 Terminology and Classification Committee.

The American Association on Intellectual and Developmental Disabilities (AAIDD) has updated the definition of ID (formerly mental retardation) 11 times since 1908. Each update has reflected the then-current understanding of the phenomenon and practices related to its definition and diagnosis. In the past three decades, there have been significant changes in our understanding of ID and best practices regarding its diagnosis, classification, and amelioration through systems of supports. In that regard, the 1992 manual (Luckasson et al.) went from simply defining and classifying individuals to: moving the diagnostic process away from deficits identified solely on the basis of an intelligence test score, contextualizing diagnosis and classification within systems of individualized supports, and shifting from an emphasis on providing programs to people with ID to an emphasis on designing and delivering individualized supports. The 2002 manual (Luckasson et al.) extended the 1992 system by providing more explicit criteria for diagnosis and classification, and expanded on the use of clinical judgment in those processes. At the same time, the 2002 system retained an emphasis on assessment for multiple purposes, a functional orientation, and the supports paradigm.

The 2010 manual (Schalock et al.) continues to describe best practices related to a systematic approach to the diagnosis, classification, and provision of individualized supports to persons with ID. The approach is based on current knowledge regarding the etiology of ID and an ecological model of disability, recent developments in the assessment of intellectual functioning and adaptive behavior, and a multidimensional framework that is used to both explain the phenomenon of ID and as a basis for assessment, classification, and developing individualized systems of supports.

This edition of the *User's Guide* accompanies the 11th edition of the *AAIDD Manual: Intellectual Disability: Definition, Classification, and Systems of Supports*. The guide builds on the previous *User's Guide* that was used widely as a practical resource to accompany the 10th edition of the AAIDD manual. Through the guide's chapters, the reader will find:

- An overview of the 2010 AAIDD System as described more fully in the manual
- A discussion of the relevance of the 2010 AAIDD System to professionalism and professional responsibilities

- Best-practice procedures and guidelines regarding the diagnosis of ID
- Applications for clinicians, educators, organizations providing supports, policy-makers, family members and advocates, and health care professionals

In addition, at the end of each chapter readers will find Application Key Points that provide a quick overview and summary of the main ideas discussed in the respective chapter. A glossary is also provided at the end of the guide that defines important terms and concepts.

This edition of the *User's Guide* has been developed to assist professionals in the field of ID to understand and apply the 2010 AAIDD System. The intent is not to repeat the considerable conceptual and scientific details found in the 2010 manual. Rather, our primary purposes are to provide an overview of the key features of the 2010 system, tie the system to public policies and best practices affecting service delivery trends in the field, and show how one's use of the various components of the 2010 system can help one understand the dynamic nature of ID and thereby enhance the effectiveness and quality of policies, practices, and valued personal outcomes.

LIST OF TABLES

Table 2.1	Professional Responsibilities in Diagnosis: Assessment of Intellectual Functioning
Table 2.2	Professional Responsibilities in Diagnosis: Assessment of Adaptive Behavior
Table 2.3	Professional Responsibilities in Classification
Table 2.4	Professional Responsibilities in Planning Supports
Table 3.1	Characteristics of Persons with ID with Higher IQ Scores
Table 3.2	Significant Limitations in Adaptive Behavior: A Summary of the Research
Table 3.3	Guidelines for Synthesizing Obtained Information
Table 3.4	Guidelines for Making a Retrospective Diagnosis
Table 5.1	Components of Systems of Supports
Table 5.2	Relationship between Quality of Life Domains and UN Convention Articles
Table 6.1	Person-Referenced Outcome Domains and Exemplary Indicators
Table 6.2	Person-Referenced Outcomes from AAIDD Framework Subsumed under the Four Goals of Disability Policy
Table 6.3	Family-Related Outcome Domains and Exemplary Indicators
Table 6.4	Societal Outcome Domains and Exemplary Indicators

List of Figures

Figure 1.1 Theoretical framework of human functioning.

Figure 4.1 Program planning matrix for Jacob.

Figure 4.2 Team roles and responsibilities form for Jacob.

Figure 5.1 A systems approach to the supports model.

Chapter 1
Overview of the 2010 AAIDD Definition, Classification, and Systems of Supports

Definition of Intellectual Disability and Assumptions Regarding its Implementation

> Intellectual disability (ID) is characterized by significant limitations both in intellectual functioning and in adaptive behavior as expressed in conceptual, social, and practical adaptive skills. This disability originates before age 18. The following five assumptions are essential to the application of this definition:
>
> 1. Limitations in present functioning must be considered within the context of community environments typical of the individual's age peers and culture.
> 2. Valid assessment considers cultural and linguistic diversity as well as differences in communication, sensory, motor, and behavioral factors.
> 3. Within an individual, limitations often coexist with strengths.
> 4. An important purpose of describing limitations is to develop a profile of needed supports.
> 5. With appropriate supports over a sustained period, the life functioning of the person with intellectual disability generally will improve.

Operationalizing the Definition

- The "significant limitations in intellectual functioning" criterion for the diagnosis of ID is an IQ score that is approximately two standard deviations below the mean, considering the standard error of measurement for the specific instruments used and the instruments' strengths and limitations.
- The "significant limitations in adaptive behavior" criterion is operationalized as performance that is approximately two standard deviations below the mean of either (1) one of the following three types of adaptive behavior: conceptual, social, or practical, or (2) an overall score on a standardized measure of conceptual, social, and practical skills. The assessment instruments' standard error of measurement and the instruments' strengths and limitations must be considered when interpreting the individual's obtained score.
- The age of onset criterion is that the disability originates before age 18.

The Multidimensionality of ID: The 2010 System's Conceptual Framework of Human Functioning

A multidimensional model of human functioning was first proposed in the 1992 manual (Luckasson et al.) and refined in the 2002 manual (Luckasson et al.). A further refinement is shown in Figure 1.1. As shown in the figure, the conceptual framework of human functioning has three major components: five dimensions (intellectual abilities, adaptive behavior, health, participation, and context); a depiction of the interactive role that supports play in human functioning; and the dynamic nature of human functioning. As a brief overview:

- **Intelligence** is a general mental capacity that includes reasoning, planning, solving problems, thinking abstractly, comprehending complex ideas, learning quickly, and learning from experience.
- **Adaptive behavior** is the collection of conceptual, social, and practical skills that have been learned and are performed by people in their everyday lives.
- **Health** is a state of complete physical, mental, and social well-being.
- **Participation** refers to roles and interactions in the areas of home living, work, education, leisure, spiritual, and cultural activities.
- **Context** describes the interrelated conditions within which people live their everyday lives. Contextual factors include environmental factors (such as physical, social, and attitudinal environment) and personal factors (such as gender, race, age, motivation, lifestyle, habits, coping styles, and social background).
- **Supports** are resources and strategies that aim to promote the development, education, interests, and personal well-being of a person and enhance individual functioning.
- **Human functioning** is an umbrella term for all life activities and encompasses body structures and functions, personal activities, and participation. These in turn are influenced by one's health and environmental and contextual factors.

The framework of human functioning depicted in Figure 1.1 recognizes that although the *diagnosis of ID* involves intellectual functioning, adaptive behavior, and age of origination, the *expression of ID* in relation to human functioning involves the dynamic, reciprocal engagement among intellectual ability, adaptive behavior, health, participation, context, and individualized supports. The implication is that whereas the life functioning of the individual with ID can improve with personalized and sustained supports, a valid diagnosis of ID will not change.

Framework for Assessment

Assessment in the field of ID is conducted to diagnose a disability, classify by relevant disability aspects, and plan for individualized needed supports. To achieve specific assessment purposes, three criteria need to be met: (1) the assessment tools and process should match the purpose for the assessment, (2) the assessment findings should be as valid as possible, and (3) the results should be both useful and purposefully applied. As summarized below, best practices in assessment align the assessment function with the specific purpose(s) and the measures, tools, and assessment methods used.

- **Assessment Function: Diagnosis**
  - Specific purpose(s): establish presence or absence of ID or establish eligibility for services, benefits, and/or legal protections

Overview of the 2010 AAIDD Definition

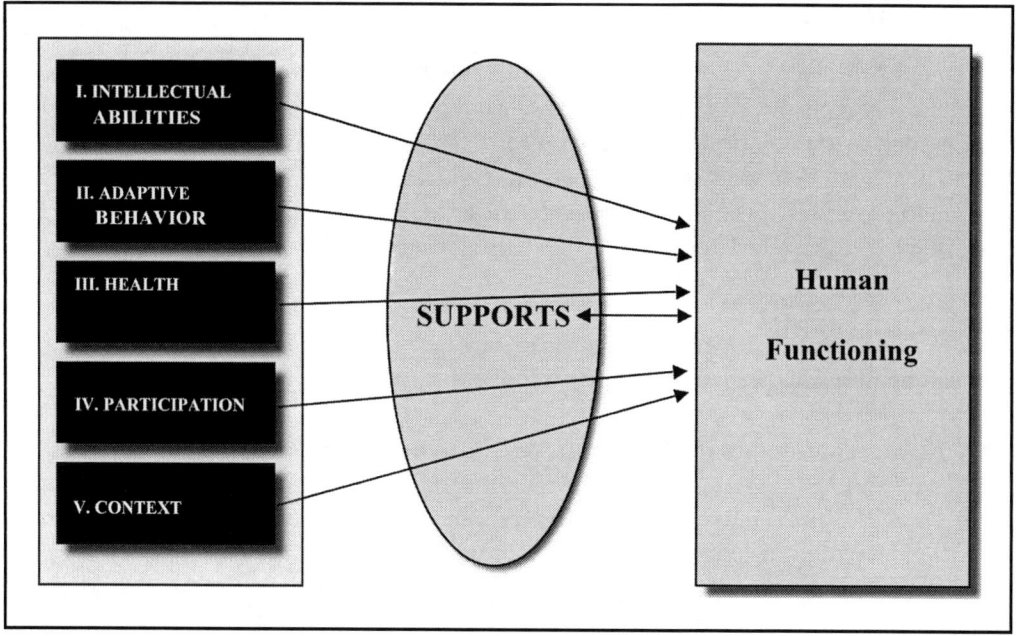

Figure 1.1. Theoretical framework of human functioning.

- Examples of measures, tools, and assessment methods: intelligence tests, adaptive behavior scales, documented age of onset, developmental measures, social and medical history, and educational records
- **Assessment Function: Classification**
  - Specific purpose(s): classify for intensity of needed supports, research purposes, special education supports, and/or reimbursement/funding levels
  - Examples of measures, tools, and assessment methods: support needs intensity scales, levels of adaptive behavior, IQ ranges or levels, environmental assessment, etiology-risk factor systems, mental health measures, benefit categories
- **Assessment Function: Planning and Developing Systems of Supports**
  - Specific purpose(s): support to enhance human functioning, improve outcomes, help implement personal choices, and/or assure human rights
  - Examples of measures, tools, and assessment methods: person-centered planning, self-appraisal, ecological inventories, developmental tests, speech/language, motor or sensory assessments, achievement tests, support needs intensity scales, functional behavioral assessment, behavior support plan, family-centered support plan, individual supports plan, self-directed plan

MULTIFACTORIAL APPROACH TO ETIOLOGY

As with the 1992 and 2002 systems, the 2010 system presents a multifactorial approach to etiology that organizes the causal factors related to ID into *types of risk factors* and *timing of those factors*. This multifactorial approach allows one to describe all of the risk factors that contribute to the individual's present functioning and thereby identify strategies for supporting the individual and family to ameliorate those risk factors.

Types of Risk Factors

The types of risk factors include: (1) biomedical factors related to biologic processes such as genetic disorders or poor nutrition, (2) social factors related to social and family interactions such as stimulation and adult responsiveness, (3) behavioral factors related to potentially causal behaviors such as dangerous (injurious) activities or maternal substance abuse, and (4) educational factors related to the availability of learning supports that promote intellectual development and the development of adaptive skills.

Timing of Factors

Risk can be prenatal, perinatal, or postnatal. Examples listed by risk factor include:

- *Prenatal*: chromosomal disorder, poverty, parental drug use, lack of preparation for parenthood
- *Perinatal:* birth injury, lack of access to prenatal care, parental rejection of caretaking, lack of knowledge about intervention or treatment
- *Postnatal*: traumatic brain injury, impaired child–caregiver interaction, child abuse and neglect, delayed diagnosis

FRAMEWORK FOR SUPPORTS

Throughout the 2010 manual, supports are defined as resources and strategies that aim to promote the development, education, interests, and well-being of the person, and that enhance individual functioning and personal outcomes. Best practices regarding the provision of supports are:

- The provision of supports should be based on a standardized assessment of the pattern and intensity of supports necessary for a person to function as effectively as possible compared to normative human functioning.
- Individual support plans should: (1) be based on personal goals and assessed support needs; (2) include systems of supports whose key components are incentives, cognitive supports, tools (e.g., AT and IT), environmental accommodation, skills/knowledge, and inherent ability; and (3) be monitored in regard to processes and evaluated in regard to personal outcomes. Systems of supports are discussed in Chapter 5 (see, esp., Table 5.1).

IMPORTANCE OF CLINICAL JUDGMENT

The 2010 system embraces the importance of clinical judgment and expands our understanding of its use as a critical part of professionalism and professional responsibilities. Clinical judgment is considered to be a special type of judgment rooted in a high level of clinical expertise and experiences that emerge directly from extensive data. It is based on the clinician's explicit training, direct experiences with the person with whom the clinician is working, and specific knowledge of the person and his/her environment.

Clinical judgment is characterized by its being systematic (i.e., organized, sequential, and logical), formal (i.e., explicit and reasoned), and transparent (i.e., apparent and communicated clearly). Valid clinical judgment is based on four clinical judgment strategies that are described in more detail in Chapter 3 of this guide: (1) clarifying and stating precisely the question set before the clinician, and determining whether the question relates to diagnosis, classification, or planning supports; (2) conducting or accessing a thorough history; (3) conducting or accessing broad-based assessments; and (4) synthesizing the obtained information.

RELATION TO OTHER SYSTEMS

The 2010 system is compatible with other diagnostic and classification systems. For example, the definition of ID/mental retardation presented in the 1968, 1980, 1987, 1994, and 2000 American Psychiatric Association's (APA) *Diagnostic and Statistical Manual of Mental Disorders* (4th ed., text rev.) mirror those published by AAIDD/AAMR in comparable years (see Table 1.1, pages 8–9 in Schalock et al., 2010). Second, both the World Health Organization (2001) in its ICF Model and the 2010 AAIDD System have adopted a dual approach to answering the question, "What is a disability?" Both systems are functional and ecological in their conceptual models, recognize the biomedical aspects of disablement, and stress the multidimensionality of disablement. In addition, there is congruence between the adaptive skill areas found in the 2010 AAIDD System and the activity and participation domains found in the ICF Model. The two approaches differ in three important respects: (1) the ICF Model is a general model of disability, whereas the 2010 AAIDD System is specific to ID; (2) the ICF reflects an epidemiological view of functioning and disability, whereas the 2010 AAIDD System includes subjective aspects of functioning (e.g., personal appraisal and subjective well-being), and a strong orientation toward individualized supports; and (3) the 2010 AAIDD System does not provide specific diagnostic or classification codes.

APPLICATION KEY POINTS

1. **The diagnosis of ID requires the demonstration of significant limitations in intellectual functioning and adaptive behavior and age of onset prior to age 18.**
2. **The expression of ID can best be understood on the basis of a multidimensional model of human functioning that involves the dynamic, reciprocal engagement among intellectual abilities, adaptive behavior, health, participation, context, and individualized supports.**
3. **The etiology of ID can best be explained on the basis of multiple risk factors that can occur prenatally, perinatally, or postnatally.**
4. **Best practices include the planning and provision of individualized supports based on the assessment of individual support needs and their intensity and provided through systems of supports.**
5. **The 2010 AAIDD System is compatible with other diagnostic and classification systems.**

Chapter 2

Relevance of the 2010 AAIDD System to Professionalism and Professional Responsibilities

Introduction and Overview

Fulfilling one's professional responsibilities is among the highest, if not the highest, goal of a member of a profession. Being well trained in current best practices of one's profession, maintaining professional standards, and abiding by the code of ethics are all necessary but not sufficient conditions in meeting one's professional responsibilities. This is because professionals working in the intellectual disability (ID) field frequently encounter situations involving diagnosis, classification, and supports planning that require extensive data obtained from multiple sources, specialized training in assessment and test interpretation, familiarity with public policy and public laws, direct experience with those with whom the professional is working, and specific knowledge of the person with ID. In addition, this responsibility typically becomes more apparent where there is a difficult or complex case and when standard professional practices are insufficient. The term *clinical judgment* refers to the special type of judgment that is required in such cases to fulfill one's professional responsibility, and to enhance the quality, validity, and precision of the professional's decision or recommendation in that case.

This chapter has two primary purposes. The first purpose is to briefly summarize the four components of professionalism and professional responsibilities: best practices, professional standards, professional ethics, and clinical judgment. The second purpose is to summarize professional responsibilities in diagnosis, classification, and planning supports.

Four Components of Professionalism and Professional Responsibilities

Best Practices

The 2010 manual summarizes best practices related to defining, diagnosing, classifying, and planning individualized supports for persons with ID. Chief among these best practices are:

- Distinguishing between an operational and constitutive definition of ID. An operational definition defines ID on the basis of how it is observed and measured. Three criteria are used to define ID operationally: significant limitations in intellectual functioning, significant limitations in adaptive behavior, and age of onset before age 18. A constitutive definition of ID defines the phenomenon in relation to other constructs such as a social-ecological model of disability, a multidimensional model of human functioning, and the role of supports (see Figure 1.1).
- Aligning the clinical functions of diagnosis, classification, and developing a system of supports. As summarized in the preceding chapter, this alignment is based on a framework for assessment that shows clearly the logical relationships among the

assessment function (diagnosis, classification, and supports planning), the specific purpose for the assessment, and examples of measures, tools, and assessment methods that can be used.
- Recognizing the multifactorial nature of the etiology of ID (risk factors and the timing of those factors).
- Using a multidimensional approach to classification that is based on the specific purpose for classification and incorporates the factors that impact human functioning (see Figure 1.1).
- Basing systems of supports on a standardized assessment of the pattern and intensity of supports needed to increase the individual's functioning, to be successful in major life activities, and/or to maintain or improve one's medical condition and/or minimize one's exceptional behavioral needs.

Professional Standards

Each profession publishes professional standards that provide the basis for evaluating practices and personnel preparation, and are used typically for accreditation or quality control. Additionally, professional standards are used as a measure against which to compare individual professional performance and/or as criteria to review professional behavior and enforce rules of conduct. As discussed more fully in Schalock and Luckasson (2005), a number of typical professional standards relate directly to diagnosis, classification, and systems of supports situations. These include:

- using current information and valid information gathering strategies
- using judgment that is consistent with professional standards
- respecting client and professional relationships
- using consent (including the elements of capacity, information, and voluntariness)
- using personal information properly
- recognizing any conflicts of interest

Professional Ethics

Most ethical guidelines can be integrated into the following five ethical principles: exhibits competence, exhibits professional and scientific responsibility, shows respect for peoples' rights and dignity, exhibits concern for others' welfare, and contributes to community and society. Although each profession may define these principles slightly differently, these five principles collectively encompass well the purpose of a profession having a set of ethical principles, which is to describe a system of moral behavior and the rules of conduct recognized in respect to a particular class of human actions or a particular group. The following three ethical principles reflect the judgments of value and obligation that are at the heart of professional ethics:

- justice (treating all people equitably)
- beneficence (doing good)
- autonomy (reflecting the authority of every person to control actions that primarily affect him- or herself)

Clinical Judgment

Clinical judgment is a special type of judgment rooted in a high level of clinical expertise and experience; it emerges directly from extensive data. It is based on the clinician's explicit training, direct experience with those with whom the clinician is working, and specific knowledge of the person and the person's environment.

- Clinical judgment is characterized by its being systematic (i.e., organized, sequential, and logical), formal (i.e., explicit and reasoned), and transparent (i.e., apparent and communicated clearly).
- The overall purpose of clinical judgment is to enhance the quality, validity, and precision of the clinician's decision or recommendation in a particular case. In addition, the use of clinical judgment strategies leads to more transparent analyses and increasingly logical and principled decisions and recommendations.
- Clinical judgment should not be thought of as justification for abbreviated evaluation, a vehicle for stereotypes or prejudice, a substitute for insufficiently explored questions, an excuse for incomplete or missing data, or a way to solve political problems.
- Clinical judgment is used in the field of ID for actions related to diagnosis, classification, and/or planning individualized supports. In these situations, clinical judgment is operationalized through the use of clinical judgment strategies that enhance the quality, validity, and precision of the clinician's decision or recommendation in a particular case. Increased levels of clinical judgment are required especially in those complex diagnosis, classification, and systems of support situations in which the complexity of the person's functioning precludes standardized assessment, legal restrictions significantly reduce opportunities to observe and assess the person, historical information is missing or cannot be obtained, there are serious questions about the validity of the data, or a retrospective diagnosis is required.

PROFESSIONAL RESPONSIBILITIES IN DIAGNOSIS, CLASSIFICATION, AND PLANNING SUPPORTS

The four components of professionalism and professional responsibilities just summarized should be integrated into the specific actions and behaviors of clinicians and others in their work with individuals with ID. The following four tables summarize these professional responsibilities as they relate to the clinical functions of diagnosis, classification, and planning supports.

TABLE 2.1

Professional Responsibilities in Diagnosis: Assessment of Intellectual Functioning

1.	Use individually administered, standardized instrument(s) that yield a measure of general intellectual functioning.
2.	Select specific standardized measure(s) that can accommodate the person's cultural and linguistic diversity.
3.	Use the most recent norms of the assessment instruments selected to measure intellectual functioning.
4.	Interpret the person's IQ score(s) considering: (a) a statistical confidence interval based on the standard error of measurement for the specific instrument used, and (b) the instruments' strengths and limitations.
5.	Consider any potential influence, both positive and negative, of personal characteristics, environmental factors, and practice effects on test results.

TABLE 2.2

Professional Responsibilities in Diagnosis: Assessment of Adaptive Behavior

1.	Use individually administered instrument(s) that yield a measure of conceptual, social, and practical adaptive skills, or an overall score/measure of conceptual, social, and practical adaptive skills.
2.	Use direct observation(s) of adaptive behavior.
3.	Use trained professional interviewers and respondents who: (a) understand the principles of adaptive behavior (such as the fact that it is typical behavior not maximal behavior), (b) use age peers who live in the community as the comparison group, (c) know the individual being assessed very well, and (d) have had the opportunity to observe the person on a daily or weekly basis across multiple environments.
4.	Employ adaptive behavior assessment instrument(s) that have been normed within community environments on individuals who are of the same age as the individual being evaluated.

TABLE 2.2 (*continued*)

5.	Interpret the person's adaptive behavior score(s) considering: (a) a statistical confidence interval based on the standard error of measurement for the specific instrument used, and (b) the instruments' strengths and limitations.
6.	Self-ratings may contain a certain degree of bias and should be interpreted with caution when determining an individual's level of adaptive behavior.
7.	The interpretation of an adaptive behavior score should include: (a) the potential influence of specific sensory, motor, or communication limitations; and (b) the identification of factors that influence adaptive behavior functioning and consequent scores such as opportunities, environments typical of the individual's age peers, and socio-cultural considerations.

TABLE 2.3

Professional Responsibilities in Classification

1.	Any classification system used should be justified by a specific rationale, purpose, and intended use.
2.	Non-stigmatizing classification systems should be used.
3.	Any age-referenced term (such as mental age or developmental age) should be used cautiously, if at all, and only in those rare situations in which the stigmatizing term is necessary for meaningful communication.
4.	A multidimensional classification system whose components include the five dimensions, supports, and human functioning (see Figure 1.1) can provide the most comprehensive and useful information about the person.

TABLE 2.4

Professional Responsibilities in Planning Supports

1.	Supports should be integrated within the five dimensions of human functioning: intellectual abilities, adaptive behavior, health, participation, and context.
2.	Supports should be based on a standardized assessment of the person's support needs across life activity areas and in reference to exceptional medical and behavioral support needs.
3.	Support planning should be based on the person's life experiences and goals.
4.	Support provision should be based on systems of supports (see Table 5.1).

© American Association on Intellectual and Developmental Disabilities

APPLICATION KEY POINTS

1. Professionalism and professional responsibilities in the field of ID involve demonstrating best practices, maintaining professional standards, abiding by a code of ethics, and using informed clinical judgment that is based on training, experience, and knowledge of research-based information.

2. Clinical judgment strategies, when properly applied, enhance the quality, validity, and precision of the clinician's decision or recommendation. The use of clinical judgment strategies is especially necessary in complex diagnostic, classification, and planning supports situations in which the complexity of the person's functioning precludes standardized assessment, legal restrictions significantly reduce opportunities to observe and assess the person, historical information is missing or cannot be obtained, there are serious questions about the validity of the data, or a retrospective diagnosis is required.

3. Professional responsibilities in diagnosis involve the use of individually administered, standardized instruments that assess intellectual functioning or adaptive behavior.
   - Both types of instruments should be: appropriate to the person's age and culture, normed on age peers within community environments, and interpreted within the context of personal and environmental factors.
   - The interpretation of both an individual's IQ score and adaptive behavior score should include the standard error of measurement for the specific instrument used and the instruments' strengths and limitations.
   - The adaptive behavior assessment should yield a measure of conceptual, social, and practical adaptive skills.

4. Professional responsibilities in classification involve dividing into subgroups based on a clear rationale regarding the classification's purpose and intended outcomes. Furthermore, a multidimensional classification system provides the most comprehensive and most useful information about the person.

5. Professional responsibilities in planning supports involve basing systems of supports on the individual's support needs as assessed on a standardized support needs scale.

Chapter 3

Applications for Clinicians in the Diagnosis of Intellectual Disability

Introduction and Overview

Members of a variety of professions, such as psychologists, physicians, diagnosticians, expert educators, special education teachers, and social workers are frequently involved in the diagnosis, classification, and planning and/or providing supports to persons with intellectual disability (ID). These individuals are members of their primary profession and may also be members of the unique interdisciplinary group of ID professionals. These individuals can be categorized as "clinicians in intellectual disability" if they: (1) have relevant training, (2) engage in clinical activities with individuals with ID, (3) use appropriately the 2010 AAIDD System for actions related to diagnosis, classification, and planning supports; and (4) demonstrate within the relevant policies and statutes of their respective jurisdictions those professional behaviors summarized in Tables 2.1–2.4 related to diagnosis, classification, and/or planning supports.

Fulfilling one's professional responsibilities is among the highest, if not highest, goal of a member of a profession. Although this statement applies to each of the three clinical functions of diagnosis, classification, and planning supports, clinicians in the field of ID have expressed to AAIDD and the authors of this *User's Guide* the need for a clear set of guidelines regarding: (1) clinical strategies to deal with complex diagnostic situations, especially those involving persons with ID with higher IQ scores; (2) guidelines for making a retrospective diagnosis; and (3) how to foster justice when dealing with forensic issues that arise when persons with ID are involved with the civil or criminal justice systems. This chapter presents guidelines to address these needs.

Because most of these needs and issues relate to persons with ID with higher IQ scores we begin with a summary of the major characteristics of these individuals. The information presented in Table 3.1 is based on the empirical research outlined and discussed in Snell and Luckasson et al. (2009) and summarized in Schalock et al. (2010, pp. 154–155).

The characteristics summarized in Table 3.1 provide the framework for understanding what a profile of significant limitations in adaptive behavior might look like. Such a profile, based on the empirical research summarized in Snell and Luckasson et al. (2009), is presented in Table 3.2. It should be noted that all of the characteristics listed in Table 3.2 are not necessarily represented in all adaptive behavior instruments. Therefore, this summary is more complete than the adaptive behaviors assessed in any one adaptive behavior assessment instrument and necessitates that in addition to a standardized adaptive behavior assessment, there needs to be both a review of existing records and the obtaining of information from multiple individuals who have had the opportunity to directly observe the person engaging in his or her typical behaviors across community contexts (e.g., home, community, school, work).

Table 3.1
Characteristics of Persons with ID with Higher IQ Scores

- High rates of classroom segregation and slightly lower rates of leaving school compared to students without ID
- Lower socioeconomic status
- Low rate of employment and low career success
- Poorer nutrition and access to health care
- Most continue to live with parents or others
- Impaired social judgment that involves inadequate response systems, lessened interpersonal competence and decision making skills, difficulties in social problem solving and flexible thinking, and increased vulnerability and victimization
- Inadequate social responding and judgment as reflected in a tendency to deny or minimize their intellectual disability, a desire to please authority figures, gullibility when others mislead or harm them, and/or naiveté or suggestibility
- Difficulty in thinking and learning as reflected in difficulties in making sense of the world through consistent, reliable, socially mature levels of planning, problem solving, thinking abstractly, comprehending complex ideas, learning quickly, and learning from experience

Table 3.2
Significant Limitations in Adaptive Behavior: A Summary of the Research

Adaptive Behavior Domain	Likely Significant Limitations
Conceptual Skills	Impaired, inconsistent, or immature quality of independent planning, problem solving, or thinking abstractly
	Limited ability to generate possible solutions and/or choose a good solution when confronted with a complex problem or situation
	Difficulty comprehending or using effectively complex ideas or symbols such as time and mathematical functions
	Difficulty effectively communicating complex thoughts or ideas

TABLE 3.2 (*continued*)

Adaptive Behavior Domain	Likely Significant Limitations
Conceptual Skills (*continued*)	Difficulty in self-direction as reflected in limited ability to independently arrange or plan future life activities such as advanced job training
	Difficulty anticipating cause and effect, understanding and planning for consequences, and using logic to understand the world
Social Skills	Impaired social judgment and learning from experiences, especially concerning interactions with other people
	Impaired ability to understand and follow rules and laws in complex situations
	Difficulties in working effectively with others toward group problem solving and decision making
	Inflexible and concrete thinking and acting during complex social problems
	Increased vulnerability and victimization, especially concerning who can be trusted, whom to follow, and what circumstances are safe
	Inadequate social responding, social judgment, and self-direction
	Tendency to deny or minimize the disability to their detriment
	Inappropriate desire to please authority figures based on limited understanding of situation
	Gullibility, naïveté, and suggestibility in interactions with others

Adaptive Behavior Domain	Likely Significant Limitations
Practical Skills	Limitations in activities of daily living such as arranging steady groceries and proper sleeping arrangements, meal planning, keeping appointments, and maintaining one's medication regime
	Limitations in occupational skills such as obtaining a steady job that covers expenses, meeting work competencies, getting along with coworkers and managers, handling job conflict appropriately, maintaining high quality work under pressure

TABLE 3.2 (*continued*)

Practical Skills (*continued*)	Limitations in use of money and property such as giving "loans" to people who do not pay back, signing away property or rights, making purchases inconsistent with his/her budget/means
	Limitations in maintaining a safe environment related to one's children and self, household cleaning products, food storage, medicine/drugs, or using caution around and protecting others from electricity, vehicles, and machines

FOUR CLINICAL JUDGMENT STRATEGIES TO DEAL WITH COMPLEX DIAGNOSTIC SITUATIONS, ESPECIALLY IN INDIVIDUALS WITH ID WITH HIGHER IQ SCORES

Professional best practices and clinical judgment strategies are used to enhance the quality, validity, and precision of the clinician's diagnosis in a particular case, and especially in those complex diagnostic situations in which the complexity of the person's functioning precludes standardized assessment, legal restrictions significantly reduce opportunities to observe and assess the person, historical information is missing or cannot be obtained, there are serious questions about the validity of the data or information, or a retrospective diagnosis is required. Using the following four clinical judgment strategies and their associated guidelines will enhance the quality, validity, and precision of the clinician's diagnosis: (1) understand the question, (2) conduct or access a thorough history, (3) conduct or access broad-based assessments of intellectual functioning and adaptive behavior, and (4) synthesize the obtained information.

Strategy One: Understand the Question

The collection and analysis begins with a clear understanding of the question at hand, specifically, whether the question relates to diagnosis, classification, or planning individualized supports. Typically, three questions are asked of clinicians: (a) Does the person have ID? (diagnosis); (b) Is the person competent to stand trial, be his or her own guardian, consent to sexual activities, and/or retain child custody? (classification); or (c) What supports are required to assist this individual with ID to be as competent and successful as possible? (planning supports). If the clinician does not clearly understand the question, his or her construction of an assessment strategy will likely be flawed, the answer will not be responsive to the question, the professional's judgment will not be precise or accurate, and the clinician's integrity will be compromised.

Strategy Two: Conduct or Access a Thorough History

A thorough history is essential for a valid diagnosis. Such a history should include three components: personal/social, medical, and educational.

Personal/social history. A thorough social history should take a holistic approach that focuses on the individual's life experiences in the broadest sense, including family life, community living, and employment history. This history addresses both the circumstances in which the individual's functioning is stronger, and the circumstances in which the individual's functioning is weaker. Compiling a thorough social history is especially important when stakes are high such as in addressing forensic issues or when a retrospective diagnosis is sought.

Medical history. A medical history should include a thorough review of all records related to the following: the health of the individual and all family members; prenatal, perinatal, and postnatal circumstances of birth; any early concerns or diagnoses; all medical intervention, including the prescription of drugs; genetic or other screenings; injuries; family involvement with alcohol or other drugs; and exposure to toxins. In addition, the medical history should review all developmental disorders, physical or mental health disorders, and challenging, difficult, and/or dangerous behaviors.

Educational history. An educational history should include not only a summary of school performance and school or grade progression of the individual and family members, but also identify the outcome of any eligibility assessment(s) and whether an IEP was developed. If special education was provided, note the diagnosis (often a developmental delay label is used until age nine), the years given, and the type of placement (resource room, self-contained, separate school). Also, note whether alternative diagnoses (e.g., learning disability [LD] or behavioral disorder), placements (e.g., alternative or special school), or services (e.g., remedial reading or Chapter I services) were used that might be viewed as substitutes to ID, and that could indicate cognitive difficulties.

Strategy Three: Conduct or Access Broad-Based Assessments of Intellectual Functioning and Adaptive Behavior

The purpose of broad-based assessments is not only to answer the diagnostic question(s) set before the clinician, but also permit a full picture of an individual's functioning and thus increase the validity of the diagnosis. This information is critical in those situations in which personal characteristics or environmental factors either preclude the use of a particular standardized instrument, or in situations in which the information obtained from the initially used standardized instrument results in information that is less than optimal because of its questionable reliability, validity, completeness, and/or appropriateness.

Broad-based assessment of intellectual functioning. For evaluating whether a person meets the significant limitations in intellectual functioning criterion for a diagnosis of ID, one should employ an individually administered, standardized instrument that yields a measure of general intellectual functioning. Further, the selection of a specific standardized measure with which to assess intelligence should be based on several individual factors, such as the individual's social, linguistic, and cultural background. Short forms or screening tests are not recommended or professionally accepted for diagnostic purposes. Although the Wechsler and Stanford-Binet scales are the most widely used and accepted measures to assess intelligence, there are clearly some circumstances in which neither will be appropriate. This may be because the individual being assessed has cognitive deficits that fall below the floor of the test, has sensory or motor limitations that preclude certain forms of test presentation/response, or is influenced by a variety of cultural-, social-, ethnicity-, and language-based factors. When this is the case, it may be necessary to select among alternative instruments rather than rely on the more traditional intelligence tests.

Broad-based assessment of adaptive behavior. There are times when information obtained from a standardized adaptive behavior assessment instrument does not validly answer the diagnostic question because of lack of opportunity, lack of appropriate norms, significant limitations of the person, contradictory information, and/or cultural and linguistic factors. *In these situations, the clinician should interview multiple individuals using the following standard: the persons interviewed should know the individual well and have had the opportunity to directly observe the individual engaging in his or her typical behaviors across community contexts (e.g., home, community, school, and work).* The use of multiple respondents, consistent with this standard, will ensure greater reliability of the information obtained, and provide a broader coverage of adaptive behavior across settings.

As a broad-based assessment strategy, interviews based on the above standard should focus heavily on what the person actually does and how he or she interacts with the environment, with an emphasis on the individual's typical performance and not his or her best or assumed ability or maximum performance. As an assessment strategy, the following guidelines for adaptive behavior interviews should be used:

- Inquire about *what the person typically does*, rather than what the individual can do or could do.
- Use *multiple informants* who know the person well and have had the opportunity to directly observe the person engaging in his or her typical behaviors across contexts (e.g., home, community, school, and work).
- *Base observations on multiple occurrences* of the behavior and not a single event or experience.
- Weigh observations across multiple observers to reconcile different observations.
- Recognize that limitations in present functioning must be considered within the context of community environments typical of the individual's age peers and culture.
- Distinguish between adaptive behavior and problem behavior(s). They are independent constructs and not opposite poles of a continuum. Information regarding problem behavior does not inform the clinician regarding the person's adaptive behavior.

Strategy Four: Synthesize the Obtained Information

The synthesis of information requires critical thinking skills related to analysis, evaluation, interpretation, and inference—skills that are increasingly being recognized as the cognitive engine driving the processes of knowledge development and clinical judgment in a wide variety of professional fields. Synthesizing the obtained information as a prelude to making a diagnosis and formulating one or more recommendations is facilitated by using the 12 synthesis guidelines presented in Table 3.3.

TABLE 3.3
Guidelines for Synthesizing Obtained Information

1. Show clearly that the obtained information is aligned to the critical diagnostic question: "Does the person meet the three criteria necessary for a diagnosis of intellectual disability?"

2. Integrate information from multiple data sources (i.e. broad-based assessments and a thorough history). A valid diagnosis of ID is based on multiple data points that not only include giving equal weight to significant limitations in adaptive behavior and intellectual functioning, but also requires evaluating the pattern of test scores and factors that affect the standard error of measurement of the standardized assessment instruments used.

3. Be aware that some factors might artificially inflate test scores, thus inaccurately suggesting higher scores than the individual's true score. These misleading factors include anomalies in the structural features of the norming sample, gaps in the development of spacing of item difficulties or sub-tests of a comprehensive adaptive behavior measure, and pure error variance (Jacobson & Mulick, 2006).

4. Be aware of the potential 'false positive' (where the person is diagnosed as an individual with ID but in actuality is not) and 'false negative' (where the person's true ID is not diagnosed as such) (Greenspan, 2006). To overcome a potentially incorrect diagnosis, clinicians need to: (a) equally consider (that is, equate the relative importance of) adaptive behavior and intellectual functioning in making a diagnosis of ID; (b) factor in the standard error of measurement of the assessment instrument as well as other technical properties of the instrument used; and (c) incorporate information from multiple sources, including a thorough history.

5. When a series of scores differ while purporting to measure the same construct, thoroughly explore and analyze the possible reasons for differences in data. Possible reasons include poorly trained examiner(s), improper generalizations of test scores administered for other purposes, improper selection of tests, making mistakes in scoring, administration of the same test too close in time, using different editions of the same test and not using the most recent version, examiner bias, and so forth. For example, there is evidence that IQ score estimates obtained from the WAIS may not be precisely equivalent to those obtained from the Stanford Binet (Lukens & Hurrell, 1996; Nelson & Dacey, 1999, Silverman et al., (2010).

6. Consider possible effects of personal characteristics and environmental factors that can affect test results.

7. In the synthesis of school related factors, determine whether the assessment(s) included classroom functioning and academic performance.

8. In the synthesis of information related to the evaluation of social competence, the focus should be whether the person: (a) interprets accurately others' emotions and intentions

TABLE 3.3 (*continued*)

	based on available cues; (b) generates appropriate social strategies in response to social problems, and (c) demonstrates knowledge and use of social skills such as anticipating the consequences of one's behavior or resolving particular social problems in a given social situation.
9.	Recognize the impact of practice effects, which refer to gains in IQ scores that result from a person being retested on the same test. Practice effect gains occur even when the examinee has not been given any feedback on his performance regarding test items. In addition, practice effects do not reflect growth or other improvement on the skills being assessed (Kaufman, 1994).
10.	Recognize that self-ratings have a high risk of error, since people with ID are more likely to attempt to look more competent and 'normal' than they actually are, as well as frequently exhibit an acquiescence bias. In addition, having ID is often a stigmatizing status that is tied closely to how a person is perceived by peers, family members, and others in the community; therefore, many people with ID and their families attempt to avoid the diagnosis and thus the stigma.
11.	Do not use past criminal behavior or verbal behavior to infer level of adaptive behavior. The diagnosis of intellectual disability is based on meeting three criteria: significant limitations in intellectual functioning; significant limitations in adaptive behavior as expressed in conceptual, social, and practical adaptive skills; and age of onset prior to age 18. The diagnosis of ID is not based on the person's 'street smarts', behavior in jail or prison, or 'criminal adaptive functioning.'
12.	Recognize that a number of reasons might explain the lack of an earlier, official diagnosis of ID including: (a) the individual was excluded from a full school experience; (b) the person's age precluded their access to specialized services such as special education programs; (c) the person was given no diagnosis or a different diagnosis for 'political purposes' such as protection from stigma or teasing, avoidance of assertions of discrimination, or because of the potential impact on benefits of a particular diagnosis; (d) the school's concern about over-representation for data reporting purposes of specific diagnostic groups within their student population; (e) parental concerns to avoid a label; (f) school-based political issues such as availability or non-availability of services and potential funding streams at that time; and (g) the lack of entry referral into the diagnostic-referral process due to cultural and linguistic differences or for other reasons.

RETROSPECTIVE DIAGNOSIS GUIDELINES

The careful synthesis of information is required when a retrospective diagnosis is made. Such a diagnosis should be based on multiple data points that not only give equal consideration to adaptive behavior and intelligence scores, but also reflect an evaluation of the pattern of test scores and factors that affect scores such as motivation, sensory/motor impairments, and anomalies in the structural features of either the assessment and/or norming sample used at the time of the assessment. In addition, *the five guidelines presented in Table 3.4 should be followed in developing a retrospective diagnosis.*

TABLE 3.4
Guidelines for Making a Retrospective Diagnosis

1. Be knowledgeable of legal definitions and clarify any legal question and the form that the recommendation should take.

2. Be sensitive to language differences and culturally based behaviors and beliefs. Thus, one needs to investigate and understand the culture, the degree of acculturation, the language competency of the individual, and the ways these factors affect the person. Do not, however, allow cultural or linguistic diversity to over-shadow or minimize the disability.

3. If adaptive behavior assessments were used and reported in the records reviewed, weigh the extent to which the assessments: (a) included direct observation of the person engaging in his/her typical behaviors in the home, community, school, and work; (b) used multiple informants and multiple contexts; (c) measured important social behavioral skills such as gullibility and naiveté; (d) used an adaptive behavior evaluation instrument that included behaviors that are currently viewed as developmentally and socially relevant; (e) recognized that adaptive behavior refers to typical and actual functioning and not to capacity or maximum functioning; and (f) recognized that limitations in present functioning are considered within the context of community environments typical of the individual's age peers and culture. It should be noted that although socio-cultural factors are important to be considered by the clinician, at no time do these factors justify modifications to scores obtained by the individual on a standardized adaptive behavior scale (Greenspan, 2011; Tasse et al., in press).

4. If intellectual functioning assessments were used and reported in the records reviewed, weigh the extent to which the assessments: (a) used a standardized and individually administered intelligence test; (b) was the [then] most recent version of the standardized test used, including the most current norms; (c) took into consideration all sources of measurement error related to the instrument used when estimating the person's true IQ score; and (d) in cases where a test with aging norms was used, a correction for the age of the norms was made. A valid assessment of intellectual functioning should address these four assessment standards. In addition, although socio-cultural factors are important to be considered by the clinician, at no time do socio-cultural factors justify modifications to scores obtained by the individual on a standardized assessment instrument that assesses intellectual functioning.

5. Consider conducting a contemporary assessment if indicated in order to show similarities and changes in functioning over the life span.

Fostering Justice When Dealing with Forensic Issues

Clinicians in the field of ID may be involved in forensic issues that arise when persons with ID are involved with the civil or criminal justice system. The more common of these forensic issues center around personal competence, guardianship, property and financial management, victimization in crime, or accusations of committing a crime. This section of the *User's Guide* discusses best practices and clinical judgment guidelines that address how clinicians can foster justice when dealing with these forensic issues. These practices and guidelines relate to: (1) interpreting assessment information, (2) understanding foundational aspects of ID that are critically important in fostering justice for people with ID, and (3) overcoming common stereotypes.

Interpreting Assessment Information

There are five critical areas involving the valid interpretation of assessment information that have emerged from clinical experiences dealing with forensic issues. These five areas involve understanding the following: (1) the concept of a confidence interval (CI), (2) the concept of a cutoff score, (3) that corrections need to be made in an obtained IQ score if the score was based on aging norms (i.e., the Flynn effect; Flynn, 2006), (4) the influence of practice effects on test results, and (5) the potential effect on test results attributable to faking.

Confidence interval (CI). A score obtained on a standardized psychometric instrument that assesses intellectual functioning or adaptive behavior is not absolute because of variability in the obtained score because of factors such as limitations of the instrument used, examiner's behavior and expertise, personal factors (e.g., health status of the person), or environmental factors (e.g., testing environment or testing location). Thus, an obtained score may or may not represent the individual's actual or true level of intellectual functioning or adaptive behavior because of these aforementioned factors. *Standard error of measurement (SEM)*, which varies by test, subgroup, and age group, is used to quantify the variability that is attributable to the test itself and *provides the basis for establishing a statistical CI within which the person's true score is likely to fall.*

- For well-standardized measures of general intellectual functioning, the SEM is approximately 3 to 5 points. As reported in the respective test's standardization manual, the test's SEM can be used to establish a *statistical confidence interval (CI) around the obtained score.* From the properties of the normal curve, a range of confidence can be established with parameters of at least one standard error of measurement (i.e. scores of about 66 to 74, 66% probability) or parameters of two standard error of measurement (i.e. scores of about 62 to 78, 95% confidence).
- For well-standardized measures of adaptive behavior the SEM for obtained scores is comparable to that of standardized tests of intelligence. Thus, the use of plus/minus one standard error of measurement yields a statistical confidence interval (around the obtained score) within which the person's true score will fall 66% of the time; the use of plus/minus two standard error of measurement yields a sta-

tistical confidence (around the obtained score) in which the person's true score will fall 95% of the time. Thus, an obtained score on an adaptive behavior scale should be considered as an approximation that has either a 66% or 95% likelihood of accuracy, depending on the confidence interval used. There is no evidence suggesting that the population mean on standardized tests of adaptive behavior is increasing at a rate comparable to that observed on standardized tests of intelligence (i.e., Flynn effect). Because of the differences in test construction and administration between intellectual functioning and adaptive behavior, practice effect is not an issue with standardized adaptive behavior scales. One source of measurement error may be specific to measures of adaptive behavior and that is the concern that individuals may exaggerate their adaptive skills when asked to self-report their adaptive behavior. For this reason, numerous sources (e.g. Edgerton, 1967; Finlay & Lyons, 2002; Greenspan & Switzky, 2006; Schalock et al., 2010) have recommended against relying on self-reported measures of adaptive behavior when ruling-in or -out a diagnosis of ID.

Cutoff score. A cutoff score is the score(s) that determines the boundaries of the "significant limitations in intellectual functioning and adaptive criteria" for a diagnosis of ID.

- For both criteria, the cutoff score is approximately 2 standard deviations (SD) below the mean of the respective instrument, considering the SEM (see *Confidence interval*) for the specific instrument used, and the strengths and limitations of the instrument.
- A fixed point cutoff for ID is not psychometrically justifiable. The diagnosis of ID is intended to reflect a clinical judgment rather than an actuarial determination.

Flynn Effect. The *Flynn Effect* refers to the increase in IQ scores over time (i.e., about 0.30 points per year). The Flynn Effect effects any interpretation of IQ scores based on outdated norms. Both the 11th edition of the manual and this *User's Guide* recommend that in cases in which a test with aging norms is used as part of a diagnosis of ID, a corrected Full Scale IQ upward of 3 points per decade for age of the norms is warranted (Fletcher et al., 2010; Gresham & Reschly, 2011; Kaufman, 2010; Reynolds et al., 2010; Schalock et al., 2010). For example, if the Wechsler Adult Intelligence Scale (WAIS-III; 1997) was used to assess an individual's IQ in July, 2005, the population mean on the WAIS-III was set at 100 when it was originally normed in 1995 (published in 1997). However, on the basis of Flynn's data (2006), the population mean on the WAIS-III Full-Scale IQ corrected for the Flynn Effect would be 103 in 2005 (9 years × 0.30 = 2.7). Hence, using the significant limitations of approximately 2 SDs below the mean, the Full-Scale IQ cutoff would be approximately 73 and not approximately 70 (plus or minus the SEM).

Practice effect. The practice effect refers to gains in IQ scores on tests of intelligence that result from a person being tested on the same instrument. The established clinical best practice is to avoid administering the same intelligence test within a year to the same individual because it will often lead to an overestimation of the examinee's true intelligence.

Claims of faking. Sometimes in a contested legal case an allegation of intentional "faking bad" is made, asserting that the individual is attempting to gain a benefit by deliberately faking a disability. Such claims of faking, when they are made, are usually in cases involving mental disorders because mental illness can have a later-life onset, subjective symptoms, and waxing and waning symptoms.

Allegations that an individual is intentionally faking bad, by faking ID, occur in some legal cases. The cases in which such allegations occur are cases in which rights such as eligibility for financial supports or exemption from the death penalty would come into play if the individual has an ID (Keyes, 2004). The term *malingering* is often used to refer to "faking bad." The *DSM-IV-TR* (APA, 2000) defined malingering as intentionally and purposefully feigning an illness to achieve some recognizable goal or tangible benefit (e.g., feigning ID to be spared the death penalty). Such allegations that a person is faking ID must be analyzed cautiously, however, for several reasons. First, the elements required for a diagnosis of ID must have been present from an early age (ID must originate before the age of 18), so there is almost always a documented lifetime history, usually beginning at birth or early childhood and extending through the school years, of significant limitations in intellectual functioning and adaptive behavior. Second, in cases in which an earlier diagnosis of ID cannot be documented because the individual grew up in another country and/or there are no assessment records, a clinician may conduct or access a current assessment of intellectual functioning and adaptive behavior, including a history, to determine current functioning, and together with clinical judgment make a retrospective diagnosis if indicated. Third, the more common faking direction when an individual with ID attempts to fake is to "fake good" so as to hide their ID and try to convince others that he or she is more competent (Edgerton, 1967).

Claims of faking ID in an individual should be addressed by a clinician in ID conducting a thorough evaluation for ID using the diagnostic and clinical strategies outlined in the 11th edition of the AAIDD manual and in this *User's Guide*. The authors of this *User's Guide* are aware of the concern that some (e.g., Doane & Salekin, 2008) have expressed about the potential to feign deficits on currently used adaptive behavior scales. Clinicians need to be aware of this potential and ensure that they interview multiple individuals who know the person well and who have had the opportunity to directly observe the person engaging in his or her typical behaviors across multiple contexts (i.e., home, community, school, and work).

Clinicians who similarly attempt to use specific "malingering" tests in individuals with ID must use considerable caution because of two factors: (1) the lack of a research base supporting the accuracy of such tests for persons with ID (Hayes et al., 1997; Hurley & Deal, 2006); and (2) the documented misuse of common malingering tests even when the test manual explicitly precludes use with individuals with ID (Keyes, 2004). Standardized assessment instruments used to inform the clinician whether the person is putting forth his or her best effort (i.e., malingering) have not, for the most part, been normed for persons with ID (MacVaugh & Cunningham, 2009). In addition, recent studies have documented unacceptable error rates (i.e., false positive for malingering) when used with persons with IQ scores from 50 to 78 (Dean et al., 2008; Hurley & Deal, 2006). Thus, the assessment of "faking bad" with individuals with low IQs (i.e., below 80) should be conducted with great prudence when relying on standardized measures that are not strictly normed or validated with persons being assessed for ID.

Foundational Aspects of ID

Terminology and concepts used within one field or profession (such as ID) are frequently not understood clearly by members of another field or profession. As a result, confusion and misunderstanding can occur within the courtroom and impact legal decisions. Successfully addressing forensic issues requires that all key players understand the following foundational aspects of ID that are critically important in fostering justice for people with ID. First, limitations in the individual's present functioning must be considered within the context of community environments typical of the individual's age peers and culture. Thus, the standards against which the individual's functioning are compared are typical community-based environments, not environments that are isolated or segregated by ability or current placement. Typical community environments include homes, neighborhoods, schools, businesses, and other environments in which people of similar age ordinarily live, play, work, and interact.

Second, within an individual, limitations often coexist with strengths. Individuals may have capabilities and strengths that are independent of ID such as strengths in social or physical capabilities, some adaptive-skill areas, or in one aspect of an adaptive skill in which they otherwise show an overall limitation. Third, ID is not the same as an LD. An ID is characterized by significant limitations both in intellectual functioning and adaptive behavior as expressed in conceptual, social, and practical adaptive skills. This disability originates before age 18 (Schalock et al., 2010, p. 1). In distinction, a learning disability (LD) is characterized by a disorder in one or more of the basic psychological processes involved in understanding or in using language, spoken or written, that may manifest itself in the imperfect ability to listen, think, speak, read, write, spell, or to do mathematical calculations, including conditions such as perceptual disabilities, brain injury, minimal brain dysfunction, dyslexia, and developmental aphasia (34 CFR sec. 300.8 [10]).

The fourth critically important foundational aspect is that adaptive behavior is conceptually different from maladaptive or problem behavior. This is true despite the fact that many adaptive behavior scales contain assessment of problem behavior, maladaptive behavior, or emotional competence. To be specific, (1) there is general agreement that the presence of clinically significant levels of problem behaviors found on adaptive behavior scales does not meet the criterion of significant limitations in adaptive functioning, (2) behaviors that interfere with the person's daily activities, or with the activities of those around him or her, should be considered problem behavior rather than the absence of adaptive behavior, and (3) the function of problem behavior may be to communicate an individual's needs, and in some cases, may even be considered an adaptive response to environmental conditions.

Overcoming Common Stereotypes

Stereotypes are not unique to persons with ID. Indeed, most individuals or groups who are perceived as different on some basis are stereotyped based on the perceiver's mental model or image of such persons or groups. In reference to persons with ID, historical terminology contributes to stereotyping as reflected in such terms as idiot, imbecile, or moron. Physical appearance can also contribute to stereotypes as reflected in the statement that "if you don't have the look (as in Down syndrome) then you are not intellectually disabled." It should be noted that the vast majority of persons with an ID have no dysmorphic feature and generally walk and talk like persons without an ID.

Regardless of their origin, a number of incorrect stereotypes can interfere with justice. These incorrect stereotypes must be dispelled:

- Persons with ID look and talk differently from persons from the general population
- Persons with ID are completely incompetent and dangerous
- Persons with ID cannot do complex tasks
- Persons with ID cannot get driver's licenses, buy cars, or drive cars
- Persons with ID do not (and cannot) support their families
- Persons with ID cannot romantically love or be romantically loved
- Persons with ID cannot acquire vocational and social skills necessary for independent living
- Persons with ID are characterized only by limitations and do not have strengths that occur concomitantly with the limitations

These incorrect stereotypes are unsupported by both professionals in the field and published literature. Stereotypes are best addressed by understanding the characteristics of persons with ID, and especially those common characteristics of persons with ID with higher IQs that were summarized in Tables 3.1 and 3.2.

APPLICATION KEY POINTS

1. Members of a variety of professions can be categorized as clinicians in ID if they have the following: relevant training; engage in clinical activities with individuals with ID; use appropriately the 2010 AAIDD System for actions related to the diagnosis, classification, and planning of supports; and demonstrate professional responsibilities (see Tables 2.1–2.4).

2. Understanding the major characteristics of persons with ID with higher IQ scores helps to dispel incorrect stereotypes (see Tables 3.1 and 3.2).

3. Individuals with ID with higher IQ scores compose about 80–90 percent of all individuals diagnosed with ID. They frequently have no identifiable cause for the disability, are physically indistinguishable from the general population, and have no definitive behavioral features. Documented successful outcomes of individuals with ID who receive appropriate supports contrast sharply with incorrect stereotypes that these individuals never have friends, jobs, spouses, children, or are good citizens. However, in the rare cases in which these individuals become involved with the justice system, the system frequently does not understand key aspects about ID, thus contributing to unjust treatment of these citizens.

4. Clinical strategies are available and effective in dealing with complex diagnostic situations, including situations that require making a retrospective diagnosis.

5. Clinical strategies are available and effective for addressing forensic issues. These strategies relate to interpreting assessment information, understanding important concepts related to ID, and overcoming common stereotypes.

Chapter 4

Applications for Educators

Introduction and Overview

One aspect of life that students with intellectual disability (ID) have in common is a tendency to be excluded from general education classrooms. For example, in the United States 50 percent of students (ages 6–21) with ID spend more than 60 percent of their school day *outside* general education settings and in self-contained classrooms, resource rooms, or separate schools. This percentage is significantly higher for students with ID than it is for students from other disability populations served under the U.S. special education law (U.S. Department of Education, Office of Special Education and Rehabilitative Services, Office of Special Education Programs, 2010). However, there has been a steady trend toward greater inclusion of students with all types of disabilities (including ID) both nationally and internationally (Ferguson, 2008; Verdugo & Rodriquez, 2012).

Despite the reality that many children with ID continue to receive education outside of general education classrooms, there is widespread agreement that access to the general education curriculum is beneficial. For instance, the UN *2006 Convention on the Rights of Persons with Disabilities* approved a declaration calling for all nations to assure an inclusive education system at all levels for all students (UNESCO, 2009). In the special education professional literature, the question is no longer "should we include children with ID in general education classrooms" but rather "how do we expand the capacity of general education classrooms to meaningfully educate a diverse student population, including students who learn at different speeds and in different ways?" During the past decade, school reform initiatives such as Response to Intervention (RtI) and School-wide Positive Behavior Supports (SWPBS) have emerged that focus educators' time and energy on establishing multiple tiers of instruction within a school. Tiers of instruction are distinguished by different intensities of intervention and support, and the tiers are intended to assure that the academic and social-behavioral curriculum are accessible to all students, no matter what a student's current level of achievement might be (Fuchs & Deshler, 2007; Horner et al., 2010).

Furthermore, inclusion strategies are no longer discussed apart from instructional strategies. It is not enough to physically include students in classrooms simply for "exposure to the general education curriculum" or for "socialization"; the goal is for students with ID to participate in instruction in general education classrooms and learn meaningful skills. Students with ID should receive just as challenging and as meaningful an education as any other students. Moreover, students with ID should be actively engaged in the life of their school community by participating in daily or periodic events (school assemblies, holiday gatherings, dances, etc.), nonacademic subjects (art, music, physical education, etc.), and cocurricular activities (clubs, school plays, etc.) (Carter et al., 2005; Janney & Snell, 2004, 2011). To help fulfill these goals, this chapter addresses three applications of the 11th edition for educators: (1) educating students with ID in general education settings; (2) planning collaboratively and teaming; and (3) supporting transition from school to postschool environments.

Educating Students with ID in General Education Settings

Accessing the General Education Culture: Supports for Participation

Inclusive education or *Inclusion* is loosely defined as educating all students in neighborhood school settings and classrooms alongside typical peers and with the necessary supports for them to experience success. Inclusion works best when educational teams develop plans that incorporate the supports needed to complement students' desired life experiences, goals, and activities. Because inclusion requires that schools expand their capacity to educate diverse learners in meaningful ways, creating inclusive schools is an ongoing process. "Indeed, many—if not most—schools are on a developmental trajectory toward the implementation of inclusive practices" (Janney & Snell, 2011, p. 225). Regardless of where a school is in its movement toward the inclusion of students with disabilities, some supports may be needed by students with ID to participate in the school setting while other supports are needed to facilitate learning.

Participation supports are provided to enable students to access school settings, activities, and cocurricular programs (getting to, from, and around school) and to promote their active participation in those activities (communicating, interacting, and behaving in ways that allow participation). But participation supports also can be directed toward peers and adults to create a school climate that aids inclusion, expand their understanding of inclusion, create opportunities for staff to collaborate and plan, redesign staffing patterns to include coteaching, and create peer support programs (Carter & Kennedy, 2006; Janney & Snell, 2004). In addition, inclusive schools often make use of a range of methods to deliver special education services and supports, which include "specially designed instruction … to meet the unique needs of a child with a disability," rather than only instruction from a special education teacher (Janney & Snell, 2011, p. 228). These service delivery methods include special education consultation with general education teachers, instructional aide support, and direct or consultative related services.

> Jacob, a nine-year-old fourth grader with ID, has support needs that vary from limited to extensive. He spends the majority of his day as a member of a general education, fourth grade classroom and has a foundation of basic reading and math skills and general knowledge. Jacob struggles with activity time limits and changing schedules, and he receives participation supports to address these needs. He uses a daily schedule and movement breaks as two primary participation supports. His school has a history of successful inclusion and, thus, a supportive culture, uses collaborative teams with scheduled planning time, assigns special educators to coteach in classrooms, involves integrated or classroom-based services from related therapists, and uses a peer support program in which Jacob and his classmates participate.

Accessing the General Education Curriculum: Supports for Learning

The second type of broad educational supports includes those that bolster a student's learning. Learning supports include procedures for selecting, teaching, and monitoring educational goals and objectives. All of these supports originate with the student's educational team and typically are guided by a documented individualized educational program (IEP).

> Jacob's IEP team consists of his parents, classroom teacher, special education teacher, speech-language therapist, occupational therapist, and special education aide. Jacob will become more active on his team when planning begins for middle school.

A *program-planning matrix* (Figure 4.1) can help a student's planning team determine how to organize instruction and to identify needed supports by aligning a student's goals and objectives against scheduled activities of the school day. Supports for teaching include individualized accommodations and adaptations. *Accommodations* are adjustments to the school program that do not change the curriculum level or performance criteria in a substantial manner, but that permit a student to use curriculum content or to demonstrate learning without changing curriculum goals (e.g., adapted computer mouse, extra time on a test, desk positioned close to the board).

Jacob's accommodations include the following: (1) having his tests in math, science, and social studies read aloud, (2) getting scheduled movement breaks, (3) completing a home–school homework planner, (4) taking a communication log back and forth between school and home, and (5) using several types of visual aids (a visual daily schedule and a visual organizer–checklist for task steps in science activities and other multistep activities).

By contrast, *modifications* change curriculum goals and performance criteria. For example: "Jacob will show understanding of several primary concepts from the science unit on weather by matching pictures with simplified terms and definitions, while classmates must explain them using unit terminology" (Janney & Snell, 2011, p. 230). Students with ID and more extensive support needs typically have a lot of IEP accommodations and modifications related to their instructional program. In addition, some students will have support needs that are related to experiencing and being active players in educational opportunities; these supports might include assistive technology, assistance with physical management and self-care, behavioral supports and interventions, and related services.

Instructional adaptations should not only be made systematically and for a purpose that matches student needs, but also should satisfy two criteria. First, adaptations should facilitate a student's social *and* instructional participation in class activities. This criterion is challenging for teams to apply because it means that students are both actively involved in classroom activities and are learning (Carter et al., 2005); conversely this criterion means that students are not included simply for exposure to the general education curriculum or for socialization. The second criterion for adaptations emphasizes the importance of keeping instructional adaptations as nonintrusive as possible for the student and as practical as possible for the team (the *only-as-specialized-as-necessary* criterion). This criterion means that students are neither singled out for extra assistance all of the time, nor are students who receive adaptations deprived from participating in typical activities or in ordinary relationships.

Janney and Snell (2011) described three types of adaptations: curricular, instructional, and alternative. *Curricular adaptations* help individualize what is taught or the learning goals. For students with ID the core general curriculum can be adapted by *simplification* (decreasing the difficulty or amount) or by *altering the curriculum* so more functional learning priorities relevant to the student's daily life are selected (alternative or functional adaptations). Educational teams should not simply designate students into "simplified" or "alternative" tracks; rather, a student's learning goals in some subject areas may remain as is without adaptations,

CHAPTER 4

Program Planning Matrix

Student ___Jacob___ Class ___Bowers/4th___ Date ___September 2009___

IEP GOALS	Arrival	A.M. Work	Language skills	Guided Reading	Specialty*	Recess	Math	Lunch	Science/Social Studies	Writers' Workshop	Shared Reading	Departure
Communication, Social, Behavior												
Use simple sentences to express needs, feelings, ask/answer questions, make choices, relate recent events	x	o	x	x	o	x	o	x	x	x	x	x
Respond to and initiate interactions with peers	x	x	x	x	x	x	o	x	x	o	x	x
Use self control strategies with cues and support	x	o	o	o	x	x	o	x	o	x	o	o
Functional skills and school participation												
Follow class procedures from classroom teacher's cues	x	x	x	x	x	x	x	x	x	x	x	x
Arrival/departure, lunch routines, classroom jobs	x							x				x
Participate in individual work to 10 minutes, small and large groups to 20 minutes		x	o	x	x		x		x	o	x	
Math												
Write # 0–100 **(S)**							x		o			
Compare (=, <, >) whole numbers to 100 **(S)**							x		o			

Figure 4.1. Program planning matrix for Jacob.

Figure 4.1. (continued)

Add and subtract to 50, concrete objects (S)					x					x
Time to 15 minutes (analog, digital) (S)	x				x	x				
Measurement: pounds; inches and feet, cups and quarts (S)					x	x				
Basic bar and line graphs (across curriculum) (S)		x			x	x				
Language Arts										
Readable handwriting for name, date, high frequency words and phrases (S)	x	x	o			x o	x			
Comprehension questions, fiction and nonfiction (fact/fantasy, purpose, setting, characters, events) (S)		x	x				x	x		
Write 3-sentence paragraph (S)		x	x				x			
Read/write/spell high-frequency and functional words (S)		x	x			x	x			
Collect information from print, media, online (S)		x	x			x				
Science and Social Studies										
Conduct investigations (predict, observe, conclude; cause and effect; measurements; graphs) (S)						x				
Key concepts and vocabulary from each unit (S)		x				x	x			

* Monday: music; Tuesday and Thursday: PE; Wednesday: Library; Friday: computer

KEY: x instruction provided, o opportunistic teaching; **(S)** Specific adaptations to class activities and materials may be needed

Source: Adapted from Janney and Snell (2004). Reprinted with permission. Reprinted from Janney and Snell (2011, p. 241).

while for other subject areas their goals may be simplified or adapted in alternative or functional ways. The balance of academic and functional skills and types of adaptations also will change over time, with a likely increase in functional or alternative adaptations as students get older. Finally, Janney and Snell (2011) made a case for adding curriculum content that is "culturally relevant and/or personally interesting" so that students' educational programs include both "need-to-know" and "nice-to-know" learning goals (p. 232).

The second type of adaptations, *instructional adaptations,* is that which individualizes the teaching methods as needed by the student. For particular students, the educational team may decide to make changes in the (1) grouping or instructional arrangement, (2) teaching methods and materials, (3) task required of student, and/or (4) personal assistance provided to the student.

> Jacob's educational team determined that he learns well in small group instruction, peer partner dyads, and individual instruction; they further recommended the use of visuals (maps, pictures, etc.), hands-on practice, and concept maps when teaching math and science concepts.

One effective educational practice involves the principle of *universal design for learning* (Rose & Meyer, 2002). Using this approach during instructional planning for students with ID means that educational teams first identify teaching methods and strategies that are known to be effective for most learners in a classroom; thus, team planning begins by considering methods that have more widespread positive impact on members of the class, rather than first planning for students who do not have special education support needs and then adapting those plans for individual students with ID. Even though using universal design can create more effective learning settings for most members of a general education classroom, teachers often must change aspects of their teaching to facilitate learning and contribution by individual students with higher support needs in order for them to participate fully and to benefit from typical lessons.

The last type of adaptation—*alternative adaptations*—involves more extensive adaptation, in that the goal, the methods and materials, or the activity is individualized to suit a student and differs from those of classmates. This category of adaptation can involve *supplemental or alternate activities* to ready the student for instruction or to reinforce previous instruction. *Remedial instruction* in basic skills is a second option whereby a student is given intensive direct instruction directed toward an educational goal and typically apart from peers; remedial instruction is specialized and based on proven methods (functional communication training, discrete trial instruction in communication, mobility training). Such instruction must be carried out in ways that promote skill generalization to inclusive classroom and school activities.

The final option for alternative adaptations includes instruction in targeted *functional skills* that cannot be conducted in ongoing general education classroom activities. Functional skill instruction for younger students (elementary and middle) can be conducted in school settings outside the classroom (hallways, library, bus area, etc.) and might include (1) a school job like returning the classroom's library books, or (2) finding and navigating the bathroom, music class, the cafeteria, and the school bus. Older students (some middle and most high school) will receive functional skill instruction in the nearby community that addresses community use and vocational training. Although this instruction does not occur in the general education classroom, it is provided in authentic settings (i.e., settings that are used by people with and without disabilities). Alternative adaptations are always planned with the general education teacher so that any time away from the classroom is minimized and instruction is scheduled when classroom activities are too long or not as beneficial for the student as the adapted alternative activities.

> Jacob's team set several functional skill goals [see Figure 4.1] that are embedded into every part of his daily schedule: following classroom procedures by reading teacher cues and participating in individual work for 10 minutes and in small and large group work for 20 minutes. When Jacob was younger, his team identified functional communication goals that were both embedded across the day and addressed by his speech and language therapist through daily intensive direct instruction apart from peers.

Teams will make adaptations that facilitate a student's overall participation in school activities—called *general adaptations*—that focus on procedures that are designed early in the year and remain in place with few changes. By contrast, *specific adaptations* focus on academic content and concern the adaptations that are needed to teach changing classroom subject matter (spelling and vocabulary words, unit project for social studies, or science lesson on precipitation). Jacob's matrix in Figure 4.1 shows when instruction is provided on his specific educational goals (X), when incidental instruction is given, and when specific adaptations to class activities and materials may be needed (S).

> One of Jacob's language arts goals ["Read/write/spell high-frequency and functional words" in Figure 4.1] involves both general (unchanging, procedural) and specific (changing content) instructional adaptations. Although similar to his peers' weekly spelling packet, the general adaptations in his packet include fewer words (five not 10), only one new word per week, larger spaces for writing or tracing, items that involve filling in the blank, rather than writing sentences, larger-grid crossword puzzles, and take-home spelling flash cards. The specific adaptations are the weekly words that are selected as being high frequency and functional for him and consistent with the changing classroom units.

COLLABORATIVE PLANNING AND TEAMING

Team Roles and Responsibilities

Educational teams are central to the process for assessing, planning, monitoring, and evaluating individualized supports. At the minimum, students with ID have educational teams that include special and general education teachers and family members. When these students move into middle school they should become active members of their own educational team so that they learn to express their preferences, engage in future planning, and develop self-determined behavior. Many students with ID will require added supports for communication, movement, fine motor skills, mobility, or challenging behavior; when this is the case, educational teams increase in size and include one or more related services personnel. These additional professionals join the student's educational team to help assess, define, plan, implement, and monitor the needed supports.

Jacob's additional team members included a speech and language therapist, an occupational therapist, and an educational aide. In middle school he will become a member, too, helping to identify classes and school activities that he prefers and exploring future vocational interests.

One of the most challenging aspects of teaming is finding the time to meet. Resolving this challenge is often up to school administrators who can appropriate professional development time and faculty meeting time for team meetings, hire substitutes to rotate across classes and create time, or make use of grade level teams (elementary school) or department teams (secondary school) for such planning. In addition, when faculty receive training in teaming skills their meetings become more efficient and shorter because of their skills in agenda planning, communication, and problem solving.

Besides providing instruction, teams have many other roles and responsibilities such as developing lessons and adaptations, assigning grades, monitoring student progress, and communicating with parents. Thus, before school starts or early in the school year, teams will identify which members are responsible for which roles. For each of these roles, Jacob's team identified the team member who would have primary responsibility and the team member who would provide input (see Figure 4.2).

Teaming with Parents

Educators must remember that parents and family members are far and away the most important source of support for the vast majority of their students with ID. As important as educators and any others (e.g., friends, coworkers) may be in the lives of people with ID, there is no substitute for support, love, and commitment provided by family members. Family members are the constant in the lives of children with ID, and educators who do not attempt to form strong partnerships with families run the risks of their efforts being misguided and/or having no lasting impact.

Best practices for partnering with families call for educators to adopt a family-centered approach (see Dunst et al., 2000; Turnbull et al., 2010) in which a child is understood in the context of his or her family. The goal is to establish productive school–family partnerships that are based on mutual respect and trust. A family-centered approach calls for educators to make concerted efforts to understand family strengths, preferences, and needs, and to respect and support family decision making. Unfortunately, many educational teams have much work to do in this regard.

Teaming Between General and Special Educators

All educational teams should have professional team members from general and special education. These teachers will seek and use input from the family and student as well as from any related services team members, but their combined expertise is influential in the selection of academic, social, behavioral, physical, and vocational goals and objectives. When students have more extensive support needs, a paraprofessional may be added to the team and share some responsibility in teaching and supporting the student in the context of classroom activities. There is clear evidence that paraprofessionals can be overprotective and can get in the way of students interacting with their classmates (Carter et al., 2007; Giangreco et al., 1997). Thus, paraprofessionals must not become the sole or

Team Roles and Responsibilities Form

Student   Jacob   Date   September, 2009

Teaching and Support Team Members:

Bowers   Classroom Teacher   Conners   Instructional Assistant

Fuentes   Special Education Teacher   Ms. Johnson   Parent

Key: x = Primary responsibility
           input = Input into implementation and/or decision making

Roles and responsibilities	Who is responsible?			
	Classroom teacher	Special education teacher	Instructional aide	Parent
Developing lesson and unit plans	x	input		
Developing Individualized Adaptations Plan	input	x	input	input
Providing instruction (with accommodations and modifications):	x	x	input	
Communication, social, behavior	input	x	input	input
Functional skills and school participation	input	x	input	input
Academics: basic skills	input	x	input	input
Academics: content areas	x	input	input	input
Adapting instructional materials	x (reading) input (other)	input (reading)	input	

Figure 4.2.   Team roles and responsibilities form for Jacob.

Figure 4.2. (*continued*)

	subjects)	x (other subjects)		
Assigning grades/report card	x	input	input	
Monitoring progress on IEP goals	input	x (reports, IEP)	input (data log)	
Assigning duties to and supervising instructional aides	x (daily)	x (long term)		
Training instructional aides	input	x		
Scheduling/facilitating team meetings a. IEP team b. Core instructional team	input x	x input		
Daily communication with parents	x	input	input	
Communication/collaboration with related services	input	x (service coordinator)	input (notes, logs)	
Facilitating peer relationships and supports	x (lunch bunch)	x (peer planning)	input	

Source: Adapted from Janney and Snell (2004). Reprinted with permission. Reprinted from Janney and Snell (2011, p. 227).

primary instructor for any student; they require supervision because they are not licensed teachers and do not write lesson plans. But, they should have clear job descriptions, be included in relevant in-service training, and be active team members. Schools need to rethink the practice of one-to-one assignment of paraprofessionals to students with ID (Carter et al., 2007; Doyle, 2008).

SUPPORTING TRANSITION FROM SCHOOL TO POSTSCHOOL ENVIRONMENTS

Students with ID have some of the lowest rates of school completion, access to postsecondary education, employment, and engagement in the community (Newman et al., 2009). Students with ID (as do all students) need support in planning for the transition to adulthood. Educational teams should work with students and their families to set and take action toward postschool employment and independent living goals that are linked to the future vision of the student and their family. Educational teams must ensure that school-based instruction supports the achievement of these goals, and consider issues related to meeting standards for graduation and supporting the development of vocational skills through employment opportunities. Further, educational teams must foster linkages between students and their families and available postschool supports, including adult service agencies, postsecondary education disability service offices, and vocational rehabilitation services (Wehman, 2006).

As typical students grow older (or if they change residence) they will move from one school to another to attend schools with their age peers. Although students with ID should not be an exception to this practice, there are still some schools that have ignored the requirement that students with ID should be educated in age-appropriate and nonsegregated settings. The educational team plays an important role in facilitating a smooth movement from one educational program to the next, whether it be from early intervention into preschool or into elementary, middle, high school, or into a post–high school program. Some students also will transition from separate or private schools to public schools that may or may not be practicing inclusion; other students may transition in the reverse order. Finally, all students with ID will eventually transition beyond public school and be offered several desirable options such as jobs, community living, and postschool vocational training programs. The settings where these transition options are located will vary from being community based and more inclusive to being separate and isolated. It is encouraging, however, that an increasing number of university and community colleges offer admission to young adults with ID (Papay & Bambara, 2011).

Teams play an important part in making these transitions successful. Best practice involves careful, timely, and confidential transfer of student records and sharing between sending and receiving teams on student goals and progress, student mode of communication, successful instructional and behavioral programs, and so forth. When the transition takes place within one school district it is not unusual for sending and receiving teams to meet in advance of the move; at these times team members can identify transition goals, anticipate and problem solve potential challenges (e.g., architectural barriers, needs for peer support, difficulty with change), and arrange visits by the student and family members in anticipation of the transition. Current video-conferencing internet-based methods for connecting groups across distances mean that these same transitional practices can be easily used between teams from school systems that are separated by great distances, even internationally.

Probably the most complex transition for students with ID involves the movement from school into jobs at age 18 or 21 or whenever their public schooling ends. Often students with ID transition later than their typical peers (if at all) into jobs and from their natural home to community-based living settings. A national longitudinal study of students with disabilities found that only one-third of students with ID held employment outside the home a year or more after leaving high school (Newman et al., 2010). The amount of preparation and supportive resources for these transitions will be greater for students with higher support needs (Bambara et al., 2011; Test & Massotti, 2011).

When planning for the transition from school to adult life, it is crucial that educational teams support students with ID to be active members of their educational planning teams and involve students in the process of setting and working toward postschool goals. Individualized education planning is a process that occurs throughout the school year and creates multiple opportunities for students to be involved (e.g., assessing and describing strengths and support needs, implementing action plans for goals, evaluating progress toward goals, participating in the annual IEP meeting). Educational teams can support students to be involved in diverse ways in their educational planning throughout the school year. For example, some students might create a presentation for their IEP meeting that communicates their accomplishments over the past year, identifies their strengths, preferences, and desired transition goals as well as their support needs. Other students might be involved in collecting data on their progress toward their postschool goals through the year. Still other students might learn the different components of an IEP meeting and lead the entire meeting (Thoma & Wehman, 2010).

APPLICATION KEY POINTS

1. **Neighborhood schools are highly valued in all cultures as the location where children and adolescents receive the education needed to acculturate to society and to become productive members of communities.**

2. **Educators of students with ID must focus their efforts on assessing student support needs, planning systems of supports, and implementing support plans that will promote students' social and instructional participation in general education settings alongside typical peers.**

3. **Educators adopting a support needs orientation to ID devote time and energy to developing and implementing systems of supports that bridge the gap between a child's level of personal competence and the demands of school environments.**

4. **Inclusive classrooms and schools use a variety of education personnel to deliver special education services and supports and do not rely only on instruction from a special education teacher.**

5. **A program-planning matrix can help a student's planning team determine how to organize instruction and to identify needed supports by aligning a student's goals and objectives against scheduled activities of the school day.**

6. **Instructional adaptations should facilitate a student's social and instructional participation in class activities, and be as nonintrusive as possible for a student and as practical as possible for the education team.**

Chapter 5

Applications for Organizations Providing Supports

Introduction and Overview

Support services operate in the context of the broader social and political macro system. Therefore, organizations providing supports to persons with intellectual disability (ID) should be aware of the important principles and values that govern this system with respect to the position and the rights of such persons. These principles and values are formulated in the *Convention on the Rights of Persons with Disabilities* (United Nations, 2006), which states that persons with disabilities should have the opportunity to participate fully in society and that they are entitled to societal support to engage in all aspects of life that includes access to and participation in society, privacy, education, habilitation, self-determination, physical well-being, work and employment, and freedom from exploitation, violence, and abuse. This convention has been signed by over 150 nations worldwide and therefore can be considered a universal frame of reference for establishing disability policies and systems of supports.

For organizations providing supports to persons with ID, the convention offers a basis for expressing an organization's core values and aligning its policies and practices with national and international disability policies. Support organizations can be seen as *mediators* of the values found in the convention's articles, and as *facilitators* that enable persons with ID and their families to participate in valued roles in the community and to achieve enhanced personal outcomes through the provision of individualized supports. The purpose of this chapter is to discuss four guidelines that will assist organizations to plan, provide, and evaluate the supports individuals and/or families require to fulfill the values reflected in the UN convention. These four guidelines relate to: (1) understanding the role of organizations providing supports to persons with ID, (2) focusing their supports on the individual's assessed support needs, (3) evaluating the impact of individual supports on personal outcomes, and (4) addressing quality management issues.

Understanding Their Role in Providing Supports

The first task of organizations providing supports is to understand their role in the lives of the individuals they are serving. This role is not to integrate and adjust the individual with ID within the organization, but to use the resources of the organization to support the person to lead a valued life in the context of their family and community. Support services therefore should not be segregated from the community, but actively connected to generic services and resources that are valuable support resources for persons with ID. The mission of specialized ID services is to integrate these resources as part of the person's Individual Supports Plan (ISP).

A related task is to use the organization's tacit and explicit knowledge about the community to facilitate the person's community inclusion. Organizations providing supports therefore need to reach beyond the organization and access natural or generic supports within their community. This means that organizations must also be prepared to put their professional knowledge and experience at the disposal of generic organizations such as public or private schools, companies that hire or offer internships to persons with ID, general practitioners, residential and employment providers, sports and social life associations, and police or legal authorities. A major implication is that professionals and professional services adopt an outward directed attitude instead of an inward, facility, or classroom-based orientation. The major objective is to effectively support and integrate persons with ID into the community and to help guarantee their rights as equal citizens.

If the severity of the disability or the intensity of needed supports require specialized services, these services should engage in forms of active support or treatment and avoid becoming isolated from mainstream society. Whenever possible, these specialized support services should not segregate the person with ID from the community except to protect the person and/or his or her social environment from unacceptable health and safety risks. By addressing these two tasks, organizations are mediators and facilitators in the lives of persons with ID instead of substitutes for inclusion in society. The supports provided should therefore facilitate persons with ID to develop their potential and to live lives as close to their preferred choices as possible.

Focusing Supports on Assessed Support Needs

To help focus their supports provision, organizations need to address four questions (Buntinx & Schalock, 2010): (1) What are the problems or limitations in functioning of our clients; (2) What are the support needs of our clients; (3) How do we plan to effectively meet the support needs of our individual clients, and what strategies should be applied; and (4) Did our clients benefit from the supports that were offered.

Problems or Limitations in Functioning

A multidimensional approach needs to be used to answer the question, "What are the problems or limitations in functioning in our clients?" To be specific, was the individual's diagnosis of ID established on the basis of the three applicable criteria (intelligence, adaptive behavior, and age of onset) and were the five assumptions related to applying the definition of ID considered (Schalock et al., 2010, p. 1)? Further, did the assessment process involve a multidisciplinary analysis of strengths and weaknesses in all important dimensions of human functioning? In reference to the 2010 AAIDD System, for example, the understanding of the limitations as well as relative strengths in functioning comprise the dimensions of intellectual functioning; conceptual, practical, and social adaptive behavior; physical and mental health status and etiology; participation in terms of roles and interactions in relevant life activity domains; and contextual impacts related to personal or environmental factors.

Support Needs

Organizations need to ask themselves, "What are the specific support needs of our clients?" To be specific, was information about the desired life experiences and goals of the person obtained by interviewing the person, or in the case of severe communication impairments, by careful observation and/or consulting with relevant proxies? Was information from the professional's perspective about the person's support needs collected using an appropriately standardized assessment instrument such as the *Supports Intensity Scale* (Thompson et al., 2004)? The assessment of support needs should begin with the individual's personal goals and interests, and use a standardized supports needs assessment instrument that will reliably and validly identify the profile and intensity of the individual's support needs across major life activity areas as well as the individual's exceptional medical and behavioral support needs (Thompson et al., 2009).

Supports Provision

The key questions here are, "How do we plan to meet the support needs of our individual clients, what support strategies should be applied, and what resources are involved?" The 11th edition of the AAIDD manual addresses these questions by advocating for the provision of systems of supports that involve the planned and integrated use of individualized support strategies and resources that encompass the multiple aspects of human performance in multiple settings. Components of systems of supports and exemplary support strategies are summarized in Table 5.1.

A system of supports model such as described in Table 5.1 aligns the supports provided to the person's assessed support needs and provides a structure for the organization to enhance human functioning. From an organization's perspective, such a model provides three essential functions. First, it organizes potential support strategies into a system through which individualized supports can be planned and implemented based on the person's assessed support needs. Second, it provides a framework for coordinating the procurement and application of individualized supports across the sources of support. Third, it provides a framework for evaluating the impact of individualized supports on the individual's functioning level and personal outcomes.

EVALUATING THE IMPACT OF INDIVIDUALIZED SUPPORTS ON PERSONAL OUTCOMES

Answering the fourth question ("Did our clients benefit from the supports that were offered?") requires the assessment of the impact of individualized supports on personal outcomes. Although discussed more fully in Chapters 6 and 7, outcomes can be conceptualized as the benefits derived by program recipients that are the result, directly or indirectly, of program activities, services, and supports. At the individual level, personal outcomes are increasingly being measured in reference to the core quality of life domains listed in Table 5.2. As summarized in Table 5.2, and discussed more fully in Verdugo et al. (in press), this approach is consistent with the articles contained within the UN *Convention on the Rights of Persons with Disabilities* (United Nations, 2006).

In summary, by focusing their provision of supports on systems of supports, the organization is engaging in systems thinking and the alignment of an individual's assessed support needs to individualized supports and their potential impact on personal outcomes. This concept is diagrammed in Figure 5.1.

TABLE 5.1
Components of Systems of Supports

Component	Exemplary Support Strategies
Cognitive	Assistive and information technology (e.g. communication devices, calculators, computers, GPS, learning/memory devices, cell phones, iPad, medication dispensing devices, med alert monitors, speech recognition devices, reminders, visual aids, timers, calendars, pictorial directions, color coding of appliances)
Prosthetics	Sensory aides and motoric assistance devices
Skills and Knowledge	Task analysis, applied behavior analysis, information availability, functional/real life learning opportunities, specialized educational strategies (see Chapter 4 in this Guide for specific examples)
Environmental Accomodation	Ramps, Braille, push buttons, modified counters and work spaces, modified transportation, matching tasks to the person's relative strengths and interests, sense of basic security, adapted texts and signs, environments that are conducive to learning, positive behavior supports
Incentives	Roles, status, involvement, recognition, appreciation, money, personal goal setting, empowerment, self-directed individualized plans, community participation, behavioral contracts, opportunities to engage in preferred activities, positive feedback on performance, encouragement
Personal Characteristics	Choice making, decision making, interests, motivation, skills and knowledge (i.e. tacit knowledge), positive attitudes and expectations
Natural Supports	Support networks, advocacy, befriending, community involvement, social engagement and interactions
Professional Services	Physical Therapy, Occupational Therapy, Speech Therapy, medical, neurological, psychological, psychiatric, nursing, dental

TABLE 5.2
Relationship between Quality of Life Domains and UN Convention Articles

Quality of Life Domain	Exemplary Indicators and Applicable UN Convention Articles
Personal Development	Education status, personal skills, adaptive behavior *Article 24*
Self-determination	Choices/decisions, autonomy, personal control, personal goals *Articles 14, 19, 21*
Interpersonal Relations	Social networks, friendships, social activities, relationships *Article 23*
Social inclusion	Community integration/participation, community roles, supports *Articles 8, 9, 18, 20, 27, 29, 30*
Rights	Human (respect, dignity, empowerment, inclusion), legal (citizenship, due process, equality, privacy) *Articles 5, 6, 7, 10, 11, 12, 13, 15, 22*
Emotional Well-Being	Safety and security, positive experiences, contentment, lack of stress *Articles 16, 17*
Physical Well-Being	Health and nutrition status, recreation, leisure *Articles 16, 25, 26*
Material Well-Being	Financial status, employment status, housing status, possessions *Article 28*

ADDRESSING QUALITY MANAGEMENT ISSUES

Quality management is a dynamic and continuous process that involves the monitoring of client support needs, client outcomes and experiences, and organizational efficiency. Quality management in support services for persons with ID is not essentially different from other human service areas and involves two goals: providing quality supports and managing quality supports (Zeithaml et al., 2006). There are seven guidelines that address quality management issues related to these two goals:

1. The management of the organization has a clear understanding of the support needs of their clients and their families, and has a clear picture of customers' and stakeholders' expectations from their service.

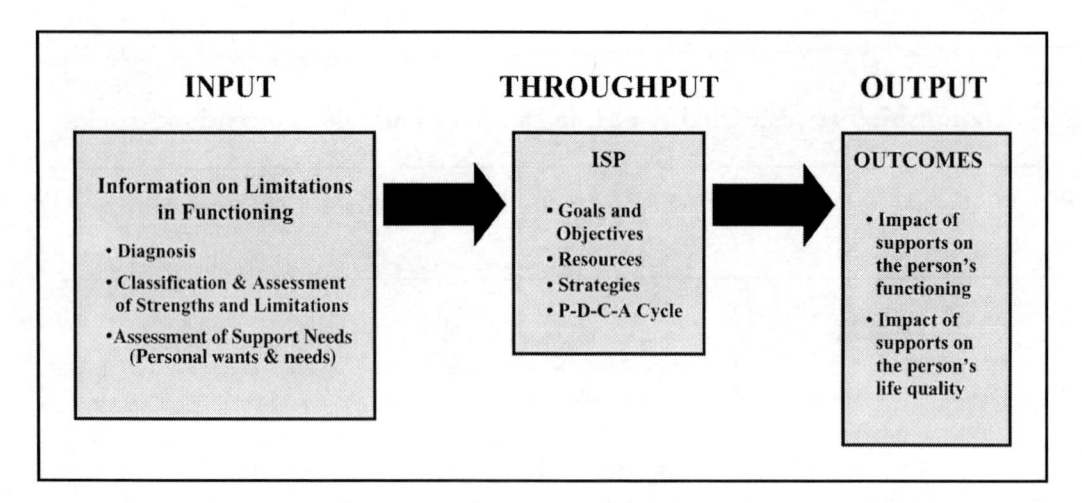

Figure 5.1. A systems approach to the supports model.

2. Supports provided are designed and operated consistent with client needs and expectations.
3. The support team that operates at the client–service interface is qualified and sufficiently enabled (in terms of resources and support from the management) to deliver the required services, the staff is empathetic to the individual needs of their clients, and there is mutual trust among client, family, and service staff.
4. Every client has an ISP that is based on the individual's personal goals, and the plan addresses strategies and resources aimed at achieving these goals as well as promoting the development, functioning, and general well-being of the person.
5. The ISP process should follow a systematic development and evaluation framework such as the "Plan–Do–Check–Act" quality improvement cycle (McLaughlin & Kaluzny, 2004). This means that the ISP starts with the planning of actions (e.g., the selection and organization of goals, strategies, and resources), must be implemented and actively executed, should be monitored and evaluated, and should involve selecting new support objectives that were achieved or changing strategies that seemed less successful.
6. The promises of the organization, as expressed in their external communications (e.g., brochures, website, vision and mission statements), are aligned with actual client experiences and real personal outcomes.
7. There is congruence between client and family expectations regarding the need for specific supports and their satisfaction with actual experiences of supports received.

Research shows that there is no simple relationship between costs and outcomes of services in ID. Neither is there a clear economy of scale evident (Emerson et al., 2005; Perry & Felce, 2005). On the basis of these studies and Stancliffe and Lakin's (2005) work on the relationship between service expenditures and outcomes, the following five recommendations for service directors and managers with respect to quality management can be made. First, provide transparent information about the supports and services to facilitate client, family, and referral agency choices. Second, make sure that an assessment of the person's support needs along with his or her functional strengths and limitations are available before actual service delivery is started (i.e., focus on the system "input"; see Figure 5.1). Also, determine whether the organization's resources are congruent with the needs and expectations of the service recipient. Third, commit to equitable, understandable, and transparent individualized resource allocation in response to individual needs and provide transparent ISPs (i.e., focus on the system "throughput"; see Figure 5.1). Fourth, develop a qualified direct-support workforce who provides support team continuity. And fifth, conduct customer perception and satisfaction surveys regularly, monitor stakeholders' perceptions and expectations (public authority and community stakeholders), and monitor client and community outcomes (social return on investment) as well as service performance.

APPLICATION KEY POINTS

1. Persons with ID and their families depend on various forms and intensities of supports to achieve the valued outcomes envisioned in the UN convention articles and overcome the challenges that are associated with a disability.
2. Organizations providing supports to these individuals and families should reflect the values found in the UN convention and facilitate the planning, provision, and evaluation of individualized supports.
3. Organizations providing supports to persons with ID should be "bridges to the community" to facilitate the inclusion of persons with ID into mainstream society.
4. Organizations providing supports to persons with ID should base supports provision on an ISP that incorporates the person's goals and aspirations, assessed support needs, and specific support strategies and objectives.
5. Organizations providing supports to individuals with ID and their families should understand their role in the lives of the individuals they are serving, focus the supports they provide on the assessed support needs of the individual, and address quality management issues.

Chapter 6

Applications for Policymakers

Introduction and Overview

The development, adoption, and implementation by policymakers and practitioners of best practices related to diagnosis, classification, and planning supports for people with intellectual disability (ID) are to ensure effectiveness and equity in public systems. As described in previous chapters, the AAIDD system establishes best practices related to diagnosis, classification, and planning systems of supports. This chapter describes how the AAIDD system also provides a framework for understanding the application of the definition of ID and its classification and supports-planning components to public policy. The public policy framework presented in both the manual and this chapter focuses on the interactive relationship among public policy, practice, and outcomes. It also emphasizes the importance of assessing personal, familial, systems-change, and societal outcomes and using outcome data to evaluate and modify public policy.

The goals and purposes of public policy and public service systems for people with ID have changed significantly over time. In the past, public systems for this population offered only custodial care and treatment in state-operated facilities. Decades later, community-based services are the predominant mode of service delivery. The focus is on person-centered services, where desired personal and familial outcomes are the primary indicator of the quality of supports and services, not program and facility needs, provider preferences, or convenience of the funder. Essentially, the field has shifted from a wholesale to a retail system. In a wholesale system, everyone gets the same thing. In a retail system, the system is disaggregated into an array of supports and services. Furthermore, the outcomes of supports and services are evaluated at the individual, not the system, level.

There is an interactive relationship among changing practices in the field, public policy, and outcome data. The evolution of public systems has created a need for updated tools to assess outcomes and for changes in public policy related to organizing and funding individualized services and supports. Likewise, changes in public policy have stimulated reform in public systems and their practices. For example, court decisions like Olmstead (1999) have emphasized the need to create community-based options for individualized supports and services outside of the confines of a congregate setting. Furthermore, data on the outcomes of changing practices and public policy influence policy and practice. As more and more data become available on the impact of individualized supports on the outcomes experienced by individuals with ID and their families, this data will influence the future directions of policy and practice.

The purpose of this chapter is to describe the AAIDD public policy framework, which provides a conceptual and measurement framework for the assessment and use of desired personal, familial, systems-change, and societal outcomes related to the core concepts and principles of disability policy. In addition, the chapter discusses the implications and impacts of the framework.

CHAPTER 6

AAIDD's Public Policy Framework and Desired Policy Outcomes

The key tenet of the AAIDD public policy framework breaks down two ways: (1) public policy is influenced by core disability policy concepts, and (2) there is an interactive relationship among public policy, practice, and desired policy outcomes.

Disability Core Concepts

Turnbull and colleagues analyzed U.S. federal laws, U.S. Supreme Court cases, and other U.S court decisions to identify core concepts that guide disability policy (Turnbull et al., 2001a; Turnbull & Stowe, 2001; Turnbull et al., 2001b). They identified three main categories of core concepts: constitutional principles, ethical principles, and administrative principles.

Constitutional principles. The constitutional principles represent the foundations of democratic government (i.e., life, liberty, and equality) that are reflected in the Constitution of the United States. These principles are relevant for all persons in a society; they can have specific relevance, however, for people with disabilities, particularly in policies dealing with the right to live, learn, work, and play in environments of one's choosing (liberty) and to be free from discrimination in accessing these environments (equality). For example, the Olmstead decision mentioned earlier ruled that the unnecessary segregation of individuals with disabilities in institutional settings violated the equal right that people with disabilities have to access their communities.

Ethical principles. Ethical principles (i.e., community, family as foundation, and dignity) reflect societal ethics, values, beliefs, and ideals, and influence public policy because if a law or practice conflicts with societal values, change will be difficult. Specific to disability policy, the influence of societal perceptions of disability and the degree to which society embraces changes in disability policy is incorporated into the AAIDD system. The AAIDD system adopts an ecological and multidimensional perspective of ID, and focuses on the role that individualized supports play in enhancing human functioning. The five assumptions in applying the definition of ID reflect this perspective of ID and emphasize the ethical principles of community, of considering strengths and limitations, and of diagnosing and classifying only to identify and implement systems of supports to lead to desired outcomes for an individual.

Administrative principles. The administrative principles focus on the capacity needed to implement public policies, the importance of individualizing services and supports (e.g., providing supports tailored to the targeted beneficiaries of policy), and the legal and accountability procedures needed to monitor policies. The administrative principles are critical to ensure that the intent of public policy is what is implemented in practice. Essentially, the administrative principles focus on ensuring that the desired outcomes of policy are achieved. For example, individualization, an administrative principle, focuses on ensuring that services are person- and family centered, not program centered.

Desired Policy Outcomes

People with disabilities live, work, learn, and play in multiple contexts. They are influenced by the environment in which they live (their family system), the neighborhood and community in which they live, and the organizations that provide support in their community. They are also influenced by the larger society and the norms that govern that society. Public policy and its outcomes are filtered through each of these environments. For example, the outcomes of public policy that focus on assessing and building supports for people with ID are influenced by the resources within a family, the resources available to the family through the local support provider, and the policies of the state and federal government related to funding supports. For this reason it is important to ensure that public policy and administrative processes encourage practices that recognize the uniqueness and idiosyncratic qualities of each person, their families, and their communities. Because individualization is difficult to achieve within complex organizations and systems, a continual monitoring of individual outcomes is critical to ensure the systems remain true to this one-person-at-a-time aspiration.

The AAIDD public policy framework identifies four classes of public policy outcomes: personal, familial, societal, and systems change. Domains and indicators for the first three outcome areas are provided in Tables 6.1–6.3. These public policy outcome classes have been derived from legislative and legal trends emerging from the core concepts of disability policy as well as changes in policy and practice, such as the shift from program centered to person centered services and supports.

Outcome data can be used for multiple purposes, ranging from assessing the impact of a specific policy to engaging in quality improvement within a state or a provider agency to establishing the parameters of best practices and the impact of the AAIDD system. Outcome data also can drive changes in policy and practice. For example, outcome data on the impact of providing personalized supports over a sustained period of time can lead to further changes in public policy and practice that reflect an individualized, supports-based approach.

Personal outcomes. The most common way to assess person-referenced outcomes is to assess indicators of individual quality of life. The eight domains of quality of life identified in Table 6.1 have been researched across cultures and time, and are commonly used to assess individual outcomes of supports and services. Furthermore, these eight domains are congruent with the four goals of public policy (equality of opportunity, independent living, full participation, and economic self-sufficiency) identified in the *Americans with Disabilities Act*, the *Assistive Technology for Individuals with Disabilities Act*, the *Individuals with Disabilities Education Act*, and the *Rehabilitation Act* (Shogren and Turnbull, 2010). This congruence is shown in Table 6.2. The indicators listed in Table 6.2 also reflect the assumption that if the individual experiences these positive outcomes, other concomitant benefits will accrue including health and wellness, robust relationships, stability, and security.

Familial outcomes. Families are a key part of the ecological context for the majority of individuals. Assessing family outcomes can also be important because family outcomes can be significantly influenced by public policy and practice. The most common way to

TABLE 6.1

Person-Referenced Outcome Domains and Exemplary Indicators

Domain	Exemplary Indicators
Rights	Human (respect, dignity, empowerment, inclusion) Legal (citizenship, access, due process, equality, privacy)
Participation	Participate in the life of their community Participate in integrated community activities Interactions (family, friends, community members) Community/social roles (contributor, volunteer)
Self Determination	Choices (daily routines, activities, personal goals) Decisions (opportunities, options, preferences) Personal control (autonomy, independence)
Physical Well-Being	Health status (functioning, symptoms, nutrition, fitness) Activities of daily living (self-care skills, mobility) Leisure and recreation
Material Well-Being	Financial status (income, benefits) Employment status (work environment, wages, benefits)
Societal Inclusion	Living status (segregated, integrated) Community access and use Connection to natural supports
Emotional Well-Being	Free from abuse and neglect Experience continuity and security Intimate relationships Friends and caring relationships
Personal Development	Education level (achievement, status) Educational environment (time in general education) Post-secondary education Personal competence

conceptualize family outcomes is by assessing family quality of life, which includes family interactions, well-being, and supports. Table 6.3 provides domains and indicators of family quality of life. The assumption here is that as an individual family member is supported in a fashion that is consistent with unique family and community circumstance, the functioning of the family and the individual satisfaction of family members will increase.

TABLE 6.2

Person-Referenced Outcomes from AAIDD Framework Subsumed under the Four Goals of Disability Policy

Equal Opportunity	Full Participation	Independent Living	Economic Self-Sufficiency
Rights	Participation Societal Inclusion Personal Development Physical Well-Being Emotional Well-Being	Self-Determination	Material Well-Being

Societal outcomes. Societal outcomes are assessed using aggregate data about personal outcomes. This aggregate data can then be compared across people with and without disabilities. It is useful to be able to make these comparisons to ensure that disability-related policies are achieving their intent of promoting equal opportunity and individual and family outcomes accepted by society. The three aggregate domains (socioeconomic position, health, and subjective well-being) are described in Table 6.4. The measurement of these societal outcomes makes it possible to determine whether the benefits of public policy have been equitably spread across cultures, minority groups, regions, and so forth.

Systems change indicators. The outcomes listed in Tables 6.1–6.4 reflect the desired intent of public policies and practices. They also represent the shift away from focusing exclusively on the diagnostic and classification components of the AAIDD system to focusing on using diagnosis and classification as a means to plan and provide individualized supports that enhance the functioning of people with ID. Data from each of the three previous areas can be used as indicators of systems change outcomes. For example, the National Association of State Directors of Developmental Disabilities Services (NASDDDS) and the Human Services Research Institute (HSRI) developed National Core Indicators (2003) that include a survey of personal, rather than programmatic, outcomes. Twenty-five states are currently collecting these data on the outcomes of over 12,000 individuals. Accrediting organizations such as the Council on Quality and Leadership (2005) are similarly using personal outcomes as an essential and integral component of the accreditation process. Provider profiles that include annual summaries of aggregated quality-of-life-related personal outcomes are being used in several states for meeting accountability and public reporting requirements and providing the basis for quality improvement strategies (Keith & Bonham, 2005). In addition, the Centers for Medicare and Medicaid Services commissioned a survey of Home and Community Based–waiver participants called the Participant Experience Survey (Medstat Group, 2003) which can be used to measure outcomes. Finally, the federal Money Follows the

TABLE 6.3
Family-Related Outcome Domains and Exemplary Indicators

Domain	Exemplary Indicators
Family Interaction	Spends time together, talks openly with each other, solves problems together, supports each other
Parenting	Helps children, teaches children, takes care of individual needs
Emotional Well-Being	Has friends who provide support, has time to pursue individual interests, has available outside help to take care of special needs, feels safe
Personal Development	Opportunities for continuing education, employment status of parents, educational level of family members
Physical Well-Being	Gets needed medical/dental care, opportunities for recreation and leisure
Financial Well-Being	Has available transportation, has a way to take care of expenses, family income
Community Involvement	Community activities, membership in groups/clubs, community relations
Disability-Related Supports	Support at school/workplace, support to make progress at home, support to make friends, has good relationship with service provider

Person (MFP) initiative includes an individual outcome survey as part of the evaluation of the program in participating states (Sloan & Irvin, 2007). Although it is important to collect outcome data, the real impact occurs when thoughtful public managers, researchers, providers, and advocates review the information on a systematic basis and apply it to improvement strategies and system reform.

IMPLICATIONS OF AAIDD'S PUBLIC POLICY FRAMEWORK

There are three major implications of the 2010 AAIDD system's public policy framework. These three relate to developing public policy, promoting professional best practices, and advancing our understanding of disability.

TABLE 6.4

Societal Outcome Domains and Exemplary Indicators

Domain	Exemplary Indicator
Socioeconomic Position	Education, occupation, income
Health	Longevity, wellness, access to health care
Subjective Well-Being	Life satisfaction, positive affect (happiness, contentment), absence of negative affect (sad/worry, helpless)

Developing Public Policy

The AAIDD public policy framework provides a clear, conceptual framework for developing public policy. The core concepts provide direction on the core values that should underlie public policy. The constitutional and ethical principles essentially state legal and moral ideals and obligations that should guide the efforts of professionals responsible for the implementation of public policies. The framework also identifies the influence of social factors and the ecological context on public policy and its implementation, which increases the understanding of factors that facilitate and inhibit the achievement of legal and moral ideals and obligations.

Promoting Professional Best Practices

The AAIDD public policy framework provides a framework for the promotion of best professional practices regarding diagnosis, classification, and planning supports. For example, the AAIDD system clearly articulates that diagnosis and classification should lead to the design and delivery of personalized systems of supports that enhance human functioning. Diagnosis and classification are not ends in themselves but, rather, are means to achieve desired personal outcomes. Diagnosis and classification were historically viewed as ends. An individual was diagnosed and placed into services that were program referenced (e.g., driven by service system needs and organizational structure, such as institutional settings or segregated educational settings or classrooms). Such placements were not based on a profile of needed supports, but instead on the diagnosis of ID and classification into a certain IQ band. However, by being aligned with the constitutional and ethical core concepts, the AAIDD system recognizes that individuals with ID have rights to life, liberty, and equality as well as a right to access community environments.

Advancing Our Understanding of Disability

Using the AAIDD public policy framework to align public policy and practice has the potential to advance our understanding of disability and to promote changes in ideology and knowledge regarding the nature of disability. Policymakers and those that implement policy must think about how they conceptualize and approach ID, and the degree to which these conceptualizations are congruent with the core concepts of disability policy. AAIDD's framework promotes changing conceptualizations of ID by incorporating the ecological perspective toward and the multidimensional nature of ID.

Public Policy Impacts of the AAIDD System

Policy Shifts in the ID Field

As mentioned throughout this chapter, AAIDD adopts an ecological and multidimensional perspective of ID. The AAIDD system recognizes the role of the environment in creating the condition we label *ID*. People with ID experience a mismatch between their personal competence and the demands of the environments in which they live, learn, work, and play. This mismatch creates a need for supports. Therefore, disability is fluid, continuous, and changing, depending on a person's functional limitations and the supports available within the environment. Rather than trying to "fix" the person (e.g., raising personal competence to levels commensurate with others), the focus in the AAIDD system is on addressing the mismatch between a person's competence and the demands of the environment. The primary purpose of diagnosing and classifying people with ID is to identify the support needs resulting from this mismatch and to provide necessary systems of supports to improve human functioning.

The focus on individualized systems of supports is effective in public systems in which services are offered to a broad group of individuals (individuals with developmental disabilities, including ID, autism, brain injury, etc.). Rather than creating programs based on diagnosis, the diagnosis is used to establish eligibility for services and supports, but the services and supports are built around the mismatch between the personal competencies and environmental demands of each individual, irrespective of diagnosis.

Although the primary purpose of assessing a person's support needs and planning for individualized supports is to create an individualized plan for delivering and monitoring supports, a profile of a person's support needs can also serve a classification function by identifying the resources needed to deliver necessary supports and services for each individual. States are increasingly using support needs assessment as a tool for resource allocation. In the past, resources were often based on diagnosis and classification into IQ bands. However, by considering each individual's support needs in the resource allocation process, resource allocation can act as an instrument for equity and systems change by ensuring that funding aligns with assessed support needs.

Role of Public Policy in Solidifying Gains

Significant progress has been made in shifting to an individualized, person-centered framework for delivering supports and services for people with ID. Changes in assessment and classification assumptions have led to an increased recognition of the importance of individualized supports to enhanced human functioning. It has also spawned the growing emphasis in policy and practice on self-directed funding, person-centered planning, and home-based supports. Such policies, as embodied in the conduct of public intellectual and developmental disability systems, facilitate society's response to individual support needs and promote person-referenced rather than program-referenced outcomes.

However, additional work is needed. It is fundamental that public policy be a driving force in solidifying the movement toward person-centered services and supports, and personal outcomes. Policies must consider the core concepts of disability policy, best practices in the field, and the ecological context within which policies will be implemented. The constitutional and ethical principles provide guidance on key person-referenced outcomes and the administrative principles associated with monitoring the attainment of these outcomes.

Instrumentalities Necessary to Maintain the Momentum

As the ID field continues to move forward, and as best practices identified in the AAIDD system become part of public policy and practice, new instrumentalities will be needed to create an infrastructure that will support a service system that provides individualized supports focusing on enhanced human functioning. One of these instrumentalities is the allocation of public resources to pay for services and supports. Until very recently, resources have been allocated to providers of services based on group rates and many times without grounding in the functional needs of the individuals served. This pattern, however, is changing as more and more pubic managers are using scales such as the *Supports Intensity Scale* (Thompson et al., 2004) to align funding with individual characteristics. Other instrumentalities include more person-centered planning approaches as well as an exploration of more human-scale residential supports including shared living. These tools that focus on facilitating society's response to individual support needs and assessing person-referenced rather than program-referenced outcomes need to be developed, implemented, and evaluated to ensure ongoing progress.

APPLICATION KEY POINTS

1. The development and implementation of public policy is a dynamic process that influences practice but is also influenced by practices in the field.

2. Public policy is influenced by the core concepts of disability policy, social factors, and the ecological context.

3. The desired outcome of the process of diagnosis and classification is to deliver individualized supports that enhance individual functioning and promote key disability policy outcomes.

4. Progress has been made in promoting person-referenced rather than system-referenced outcomes across personal, family, systems change, and societal disability policy outcome areas.

5. Resource allocation based on assessment of support need and personal goals can be an instrument for equity, systems change, and ensuring that funding aligns with assessed support needs.

6. Data on policy outcomes must be used to guide systems and policy change.

Chapter 7

Applications for Family Members and Advocates

Introduction and Overview

At first glance, parents and family members and advocates, including people with intellectual disability (ID) who are self-advocates, may presume that the 11th edition of the AAIDD *Intellectual Disability: Definition, Classification, and Systems of Supports Manual* has limited application in their lives. Such manuals historically have been principally—perhaps exclusively—used by professionals engaged in the process of diagnosing and classifying for purposes of eligibility determination, funding, and service and placement decisions. In fact, given the historic misuses of such processes, families and advocates may, rightfully, be suspect that the 11th edition of the manual has any applicability to their lives.

Although the primary users of the manual will, in fact, be professionals engaged in the above-referenced activities, it would be a mistake to overlook the potential positive application of the 11th edition of the manual for parents, family members, advocates, and self-advocates. There are a number of reasons this is so, each stated and discussed in this chapter.

Intellectual Disability is Part of and Not Apart from Typical Human Functioning

Historic understandings of ID viewed disability as in some way different from typical human functioning. Disability was believed to reside within the individual, to be a result of some "problem" within the person. Such understandings of disability inevitably resulted in stigma and, ultimately, discrimination and segregation. The 9th edition of the manual (Luckasson et al., 1992) presented a functional model of ID that challenged those historic understandings.

The 11th edition of the manual strengthens and expands the framework introduced by the 1992 manual, describing a multidimensional framework depicting ID as *part of,* and not *apart from,* typical human functioning. It begins that process by changing the term used to name the construct, from the stigmatizing term *mental retardation* to *intellectual disability*. The stigma associated with the term *mental retardation* and its associated adjectival form (e.g., "retarded") has been well articulated by advocates, and particularly self-advocates. The 11th edition of the manual describes in detail how the shift from the term *mental retardation* to *ID* reflects a change in how disability itself is understood; from disability as a problem residing within a person to understanding disability as residing at least partly in the gap between a person's capacities and the demands of typical contexts or environments.

Of particular importance to families and advocates, the 11th edition of the manual advocates a multidimensional approach to classification. Classification remains necessary to determine eligibility for limited resources, provide targeted services and supports, and communicate about selected characteristics of people and their environments. The multidimensional approach moves beyond models that focus on only one dimension of human functioning (most typically intellectual ability) to the inclusion of other dimensions (intensity of support needs, health status, etc.). The manual states explicitly that diagnosis and classification should occur only if they result in benefits to the person and/or his or her family. Such benefits might include access to funding or other resources to support community inclusion, competitive employment, or school achievement and inclusion.

The manual also cautions against the use of mental age quotients. The use of such mental age scores has historically contributed to the stigmatization of people with ID. Although there may be some rare circumstances in which mental age equivalent information is useful, the manual urges that such scores should be used for ID sparingly, if at all.

A Strengths-Based Approach to Understanding ID

The assumptions of the definition and the multidimensional framework of ID emphasize that personal strengths co-occur with limitations and that disability resides not within the person, but at least partly in the gap between the person's capacities and the demands of the context and environment in which the person must function. Further, the supports paradigm described in Chapter 5 of this *User's Guide* focuses unambiguously on enhancing successful human functioning.

This is important not only to reduce stigma, as discussed previously, but places the emphasis on promoting personal capacity and making modifications to the context in which people with ID function. The assumptions of the definition, in fact, specifically state that with appropriate supports over time, the life functioning of a person with ID generally will improve. A description of limitations associated with the person's intellectual impairment may be necessary, but only in the context of developing a profile of needed supports designed to improve the person's functioning.

The focus of a supports paradigm as described in the manual is on enhancing human functioning. This differs from previous efforts that focused on fixing or curing the person or remediating deficits. Of importance, the manual continues the emphasis introduced in the 9th edition that supports are resources and strategies that promote development, education, interests, and personal well-being of the person and enhance individual functioning in the context of typical environments.

Supports Planning Flows Logically from the Multidimensional Approach

The systems of supports discussed in the 11th edition moves the application of the manual beyond just diagnosis and classification, introducing a process by which supports planning flows logically from the model. An assessment of the person's pattern and intensity of support needs is both part of the manual's systemic approach and essential to the development of person-centered plans. There historically was limited value of diagnosis and classification for planning supports. Classification based on historic models served as a basis for placement and funding decisions, and erred by presuming that people who were similar on one dimension such as intellectual ability should be grouped together. Classification decisions often determined intervention strategies, undermining the importance of truly personalized supports.

With the multidimensional framework and supports paradigm emphasized in the 11th edition of the manual, supports planning flows logically from diagnosis. Within this framework, the mismatch between a person's capacities and the demands of the context create support needs. Instruments like the *Supports Intensity Scale* (Thompson et al., 2004) can measure such support needs, which leads directly to the design of supports and, ultimately, improved personal outcomes. As such, and unlike previous manuals, the assessment of support needs becomes a critical component of person centered planning and can contribute directly to interventions in the form of the provision of needed supports that improve the person's quality of life.

It is also worth pointing out that the 11th edition of the manual addresses both mental and physical support needs. Often, the support needs of people with ID who have co-occurring physical, mental, or emotional conditions are ignored or presumed to be attributable to the intellectual impairment. The 11th edition of the manual recognizes that, like all people, people with ID have support needs related to all aspects of health: mental, physical, and emotional.

PROVIDES GUIDELINES FOR ASSESSMENT THAT IS VALID AND USEFUL

The 11th edition of the manual emphasizes that assessment to diagnose ID must involve assessment tools that match the purpose of the assessment, provide findings that are valid, and result in actions that are useful and purposeful. The 11th edition of the manual includes an assessment framework, introduced in the 10th edition of the manual (Luckasson et al., 2002) that provides users, including families and advocates, examples of measures, tools, and assessment methods that are relevant to the specific purposes of assessment across assessment functions, including diagnosis, classification, and planning systems of supports.

Important to families and advocates is the unambiguous principle that assessment findings must be of some benefit to the person who is being assessed, if not individually, at least to the general population of people with ID. The manual emphasizes that the assessment process should be logical, sequential, and transparent, and actively involve key stakeholders (including, as appropriate, families and the child or adult being assessed). Furthermore, assessment information needs to be timely, relevant, and clearly reported.

Finally, the assumptions to the definition of ID require that assessment be valid, including consideration of cultural and linguistic diversity and differences in communication, sensory, motor, and behavioral factors. The supports paradigm requires that such assessment provide evidence of both strengths and limitations.

USE IN ADVOCACY FOR REFORMING SUPPORT SYSTEMS

Families and advocates can use the 11th edition of the manual to advocate for reform to school and adult support systems. The multidimensional framework and supports paradigm can enable people with ID to obtain personally valued outcomes such as those presented previously in Table 6.1. Furthermore, families can advocate for supports that emphasize the importance of family valued outcomes such as those presented previously in Table 6.3.

People with ID and their families can benefit significantly from system reforms that focus more on providing personalized supports, rather than preconfigured programs; provide resources that support people in their communities, instead of in segregated settings; that promote inclusive education, rather than homogenous grouping; and that promote self-determination and self-reliance, rather than dependency. The 11th edition of the manual provides a comprehensive, multidimensional framework for understanding ID within the context of typical human functioning. The supports paradigm has as its starting point active participation in typical learning, work, and community environments.

APPLICATION KEY POINTS

1. The 11th edition of the manual emphasizes that ID is part of and not apart from typical human functioning. The multidimensional framework and the changing of the name from mental retardation to ID have the potential to reduce stigma associated with the condition. The manual specifically cautions against practices, particularly the use of mental age quotients and IQ-based classification systems that result in stigmatization and segregation.

2. The assumptions of the definition and the multidimensional framework of ID emphasize that personal strengths co-occur with limitations. The supports paradigm within the 11th edition of the manual focuses unambiguously on enhancing successful human functioning.

3. The systems of supports discussed in the 11th edition of the manual move the application of the manual beyond just diagnosis and classification, introducing a process by which supports planning flows logically from the diagnostic process.

4. The 11th edition of the manual emphasizes that assessment to diagnose ID must involve assessment tools that match the purpose of the assessment, provide findings that are valid, and result in actions that are useful and purposeful. The assessment framework provides users, including families and advocates, examples of measures, tools, and assessment methods that are relevant to the specific purposes of assessment across assessment functions, including diagnosis, classification, and planning of supports.

5. Families and advocates can use the 11th edition of the manual to advocate for reform to school and adult support systems. The multidimensional framework and supports paradigm can enable people with ID to obtain personally valued outcomes, such as societal participation, and families can advocate for supports that emphasize the importance of family systems and interactions.

Chapter 8

Applications for Health Care Professionals

Introduction and Overview

Individuals with intellectual disability (ID) interact with a number of health care professionals who include primary care physicians, specialists and subspecialists such as neurologists and pediatricians; medical residents; dentists; psychiatrists; nurses and nurse practitioners; and emergency room personnel. These interactions occur in hospitals, clinics, private offices, and residential facilities. For health care professionals providing services and supports to persons with ID, three application best practices described in the 11th edition of the AAIDD manual are most relevant. These are the three application best practices: (1) use the current operational definition of ID; (2) understand the concept of human functioning and how human functioning is impacted by the provision of individualized supports; and (3) approach persons with ID from a holistic perspective that incorporates the multifactorial nature of etiology and emphasizes the individual's subjective well-being.

Material contained in this chapter addresses each of these application areas. The chapter is based on two primary premises. First, it is important for health care professionals to recognize the context from which the current definition of ID arises, and the mindset or mental models that are essential when interacting with persons with ID. There are five contextual and application factors: (1) limitations in present functioning must be considered within the context of community environments typical of the individual's age peers and culture; (2) valid assessment considers cultural and linguistic diversity as well as differences in communication, sensory, motor, and behavioral factors; (3) within an individual, limitations often coexist with strengths; (4) an important purpose of describing limitations is to develop a profile of needed supports; and (5) with appropriate personalized supports over a sustained period, the life functioning of the person with ID generally will improve. The second premise is that people with ID should have access to high quality health care that is universally available, appropriate, timely, coordinated, comprehensive, and provided within the communities in which they live. This includes primary care as well as all types of specialty care and related health supports.

Operational Definition of ID

An ID is characterized by significant limitations both in intellectual functioning and in adaptive behavior as expressed in conceptual, social, and practical adaptive skills. This disability originates before age 18.

- The "significant limitations in intellectual functioning" criterion for a diagnosis of ID is an IQ score that is approximately 2 SDs below the mean of an individually administered IQ assessment, considering the SEM for the specific instruments used and the instruments' strengths and limitations.

© American Association on Intellectual and Developmental Disabilities

- The "significant limitations in adaptive behavior" criterion is performance that is approximately 2 SDs below the mean of a standardized measure of adaptive behavior of either (1) one of the following three types of adaptive behavior: conceptual, social, or practical or (2) an overall score on a standardized measure of conceptual, social, and practical skills. The assessment instruments' SEM and the instruments' strengths and limitations must also be considered.

Dimensions of Human Functioning and the Role of Individualized Supports

Human functioning is an umbrella term referring to all life activities of an individual and encompasses body structures and functions, personal activities, and participation. The 11th edition of the AAIDD manual is based on a multidimensional model of human functioning that involves these five dimensions: intellectual abilities, adaptive behavior, health, participation, and context.

The Five Dimensions of Human Functioning

- *Intellectual abilities:* A general mental ability that includes reasoning, planning, solving problems, thinking abstractly, comprehending complex ideas, learning quickly, and learning from experience.
- *Adaptive behavior:* The collection of conceptual, social, and practical skills that have been learned and are performed by people in their everyday lives. The consensus, based on considerable published research, is that adaptive behavior is multidimensional and includes *conceptual skills* (e.g., language, reading and writing, and money, time, and number concepts), *social skills* (e.g., interpersonal skills, socials responsibility, self-esteem, avoiding gullibility, following rules and obeying laws, avoiding victimization, and social problem solving), and *practical skills* (e.g., activities of daily living, occupational skills, use of money, safety, health care, travel or transportation, schedules or routines, and use of the telephone).
- *Health:* A state of complete physical, mental, and social well-being. Health is a component of an integrated understanding of human functioning because an individual's health status affects his or her functioning directly or indirectly in each or all of the other four human functioning dimensions.
- *Participation:* A person's roles and interactions in the areas of home living, work, education, leisure, spiritual, and cultural activities. Participation also includes social roles that include valued activities considered normative for a specific age.
- *Context:* The interrelated conditions within which people live their everyday lives. Some of these conditions are environmental (e.g., physical, social, and attitudinal), and some are personal (e.g., motivation, lifestyle, habits, upbringing, coping styles, social background, and past and current life events). All or any of these characteristics interact with environmental conditions in the manifestation of a disability.

Role of Individualized Supports

The key role that supports play in human functioning was depicted in Figure 1.1 ("Theoretical Framework of Human Functioning"). One of the significant developments in professional best practices over the last decade has been to use systems of supports that encompass a wide range of specific support strategies that are used to address the individual's support needs by reducing the mismatch between a person's capabilities and his or her environmental requirements, and thereby enhancing human functioning. As described in Table 5.1, the systems of supports as presented in the 11th edition of the AAIDD manual include the following: natural sources (e.g., family, friends, and colleagues), technology based (e.g., assistive technology, information technology, smart technology, and prosthetics), environmentally based (e.g., environmental accommodation), staff directed (e.g., incentives, skills, knowledge, and positive behavior supports), and professional services.

From the health care professional's perspective, systems of supports provide a framework for coordinating the procurement and application of individualized supports and evaluating the impact of individualized supports on the person's functioning level and subjective well-being. In addition to those support strategies listed above, when interacting within the heath care environment, persons with ID generally need supports related to communication, behavior, and continuity of care.

- *Communication.* Because of potential limitations in both receptive and expressive language, persons with ID may need the assistance of a communication facilitator, the use of augmentative communication devices or systems to answer questions, ask questions, follow verbal instructions, engage in conversation, and communicate ideas.
- *Behavioral.* Because of a lack of impulse control, mood dysregulation, short- and long-term memory deficits, and the need to feel safe and secure, some individuals with ID need support in the form of positive behavioral supports that involve: (1) a functional assessment that defines the problem behavior, determine what maintains it, and describes the environmental context associated with high and low rates of behavior, and (2) a focus on two primary modes of intervention: altering the environment before a problem behavior occurs, and teaching appropriate behaviors as a strategy for eliminating the need for problem behaviors to be exhibited.
- *Continuity of care.* Persons with ID are frequently seen by multiple health care professionals across the multiple environments in which they live and work. The net result is frequently poor care coordination, a lack of administrative data to prevent polypharmacy, and confusion about informed consent and power of attorney for health care issues. Thus, health care professionals need to work jointly with the individual, family, program staff, or the individual's case coordinator to ensure access to relevant medical history and currently prescribed medication, and provide clarity of discharge instructions and continuity of care issues.

Some specialized programs have been developed to help health care professionals enhance outreach, access, intake, services, education, ability to follow medical directions, and health outcomes for people with ID (see, e.g., Ailey & Hart, 2010; Association of

University Centers on Disabilities [AUCD], 2011; Center for Child and Human Development, 2009; National Association of County and City Health Officials, 2011; Rush University Medical Center, 2011). In addition, because of the foundational role that health and disability data play in understanding and improving health care for people with ID, researchers and agencies have increasingly focused on the collection and analysis of meaningful data to improve the health of people with ID (see, e.g., Institute of Medicine, 2007; Krahn et al.. 2009; Larson et al., 2001; U.S. Department of Health and Human Services, 2005). It is essential that preservice health care professionals be trained to address the needs of individuals with ID, and training materials and resources are available for preparing medical, dental, and nursing students (AUCD, 2011).

A HOLISTIC PERSPECTIVE

When dealing with medical emergencies or a lifelong disability, it is understandable that health care professionals, as others, frequently do not look beyond the person's intellectual functioning, adaptive behavior, or physical limitations. As challenging as it might be, persons with ID should be approached from *a holistic perspective* that incorporates *the multifactorial nature of the etiology* of his or her condition, and emphasizes *the individual's subjective well-being*. To this end, the 11th edition of the AAIDD manual discusses in detail a multifactorial approach to etiology and the evaluation of person-referenced outcomes that reflect the individual's subjective well-being.

Multifactorial Nature of Etiology

In the 11th edition of the manual, etiology is conceptualized as a multifactorial construct composed of four categories of risk factors (biomedical, social, behavioral, and educational) that interact across the life of the individual, and across generations from parent to child. This *risk factor approach to etiology* replaces prior approaches that divided the etiology of ID into two broad types: ID of biological origin and ID of psychosocial disadvantage. This newer approach to etiology can be seen as fine-tuning the two-group approach. What was called "ID of biological origin" can be seen as involving individuals for whom biomedical risk factors predominate, whereas "ID of cultural-familial" origins can be seen as involving individuals for whom social, behavioral, or educational risk factors predominate.

- Types of risk factors:
  - *Biomedical:* biologic processes, such as genetic disorders or poor nutrition
  - *Social:* social and family interaction, such as stimulation and adult responsiveness
  - *Behavioral:* potentially causal behaviors, such as dangerous (injurious) activities or maternal substance abuse
  - *Educational:* availability of educational supports that promote mental development and the development of adaptive skills

- Timing of risk factors:
  - *Prenatally:* chromosomal or metabolic disorders, maternal malnutrition, parental drug use, lack of preparation for parenthood

- *Perinatally:* birth injury, lack of access to prenatal care, parental abandonment of the child, lack of medical referral for intervention services at discharge
- *Postnatally:* malnutrition, lack of adequate stimulation, child abuse and neglect, inadequate special education services

Individual's Subjective Well-Being

Subjective well-being can be viewed from either of two perspectives. One perspective focuses on social indicators that include life satisfaction, positive affect (e.g., happiness and contentment), and absence of negative affect (e.g., sadness or worry, helplessness). A second perspective, which is commonly used in the field of ID, focuses on personal outcomes that are related to the core domains that reflect a holistic approach to the individual. These are the core domains and representative indicators:

- *Personal development:* educational status, personal competence (cognitive, social, practical skills), activities of daily living, and instrumental activities of daily living
- *Self-determination:* choices, decision making, autonomy, personal control, personal goals
- *Interpersonal relations:* social networks, family, friends, peers, social activities, relationships
- *Social inclusion:* community integration and participation, community roles, volunteering
- *Rights:* human (respect, dignity, empowerment, inclusion) and legal (citizenship, access, due process, equality, privacy)
- *Emotional well-being:* safety, security, positive experiences, satisfaction, contentment, self-esteem or -concept, predictability and control, lack of stress
- *Physical well-being:* health status, nutritional status, recreation or physical exertion
- *Material well-being:* financial status, employment status, housing status, possessions, ownership

The importance to health care professionals of emphasizing the individual's subjective well-being is to recognize that when dealing with health care–related situations and emergencies, practitioners should focus not only on the intervention, treatment, or support strategy used or prescribed, but also on how one's actions will impact other aspects of the person's life. For example, physical restraint might address the lack of behavioral control, but what is the impact of this action on the person's sense of interpersonal relations, rights, and emotional well-being? Analogously, tube feeding might address an eating problem, but what is the impact of this action on the person's sense of personal development, self-determination, and social inclusion? Similarly, treating the person as "an eternal child or one whose mental age is only 3" might reflect historical thought processes and mental models, but what is the impact of this action on the person's self-concept, feelings of helplessness, participation and positive experiences (i.e., emotional well-being)? Thus, the challenge among health care professionals is to meet the unique support needs of persons with ID and provide the highest quality health care within a holistic context.

APPLICATION KEY POINTS

1. The operational definition of ID has three criteria that need to be met for a diagnosis of ID: significant limitations in both intellectual functioning and adaptive behavior and age of onset before age 18.

2. Five assumptions are essential to the application of the definition of ID: (1) limitations in present functioning must be considered within the context of community environments typical of the individual's age peers and culture; (2) valid assessment considers cultural and linguistic diversity as well as differences in communication, sensory, motor, and behavioral factors; (3) within an individual, limitations often coexist with strengths; (4) an important purpose of describing limitations is to develop a profile of needed supports; and (5) with appropriate personalized supports over a sustained period, the life functioning of the person with ID generally will improve.

3. Human functioning encompasses five domains: intellectual abilities, adaptive behavior, health, participation, and context. Factors related to these domains interact to impact the manifestation of a disability.

4. Specialized strategies and techniques have been developed for health care professionals to support access, intake, and ability to follow medical directions and health outcomes for persons with ID.

5. Systems of supports provide a framework for health care professionals to coordinate the procurement and application of individualized supports and evaluate the impact of supports on the person's functioning level and subjective well-being. Sources of support include natural sources, technology, environmental accommodation or modification, staff directed activities, and professional interventions and treatments.

6. A holistic perspective toward a person with ID incorporates the multifactorial nature of etiology and emphasizes the individual's subjective well-being.

7. The impact of the provision of health care services and supports can be evaluated in terms of subjective well-being indices or personal outcomes related to personal development, self-determination, interpersonal relations, social inclusion, rights, emotional well-being, physical well-being, and/or material well-being.

GLOSSARY

Adaptive Behavior The collection of conceptual, social and practical skills that have been learned and are performed by people in their everyday lives.

Assistive Technology Use of mechanical or electronic devices that reduce the mismatch between persons and their environments.

Best Practices Research-based knowledge, professional ethics, professional standards, and clinical judgment applied to persons with intellectual disability.

Blended Curriculum Academic and functional content are combined to meet the student's individual needs across multiple contexts.

Classification The process of dividing into subgroups that which has been included in a term through its definition. The dividing into subgroups is done according to stated principles and uses. All classification systems have as their fundamental purpose the provision of an organized schema for the categorization of various kinds of observations and a way to (re)organize information. A classification system (1) has to serve a purpose, (2) be based on relevant information, and (3) is used to better understand a person.

Clinical Judgment A special type of judgment rooted in a high level of clinical expertise and experience. Clinical judgment emerges directly from extensive data and is based on training, experience, and specific knowledge of the person and his or her environment.

Clinical Judgment Strategies A set of procedures or actions used to enhance the quality, validity, and precision of the clinician's decision or recommendation in a particular case. There are four clinical judgment strategies discussed in the 11th edition of the manual: (1) understanding the question, (2) conducting or accessing a thorough history, (3) conducting or accessing broad-based assessments, and (4) synthesizing the obtained information.

Clinician in Intellectual Disability A person who: (1) has relevant training; (2) engages in clinical activities (diagnosis, classification, developing individualized supports); and (3) uses professionally accepted practices such as those described in the 11th edition of the manual.

Comprehensive Community Health Supports Individualized supports provided within one's community that are responsive to the physical and mental health needs of persons with intellectual disability; are aligned with the current ecological, multidimensional conception of disability; and are consistent with the definition of health as "a state of complete physical, mental, and social well-being."

Conceptual Skills Adaptive skills that include language, reading and writing, and money, time, and number concepts.

Confidence Interval The statistical interval, or range, within which the person's true score falls. The results of any standardized psychometric assessment must be evaluated and interpreted in terms of the accuracy of the instrument used. Variability in the obtained score(s) can be because of limitations of the instrument used, examiner's behavior, or other personal factors (e.g., health status of the person) or environmental factors (e.g., testing environment or testing location). Thus, variation in scores may or may not represent the individual's actual or true level of intellectual or adaptive behavior functioning. The term *standard error of measurement*, which varies by test, subgroup, and age group, is used to quantify this variability and provide the basis for establishing a statistical confidence interval within which the person's true score fall. From the properties of the normal curve, a range of statistical confidence can be established with parameters of at least one standard error of measurement (i.e., 66% probability) or parameters of two standard error of measurement (i.e., 95% probability). The selection of the confidence interval (i.e., 66% or 95%) relates to the question(s) asked, the properties of the assessment instrument used, and the ultimate use of the obtained score(s).

Construct An abstract or general idea based on observed phenomena and formed by arranging parts or elements.

Context The interrelated conditions within which people live their everyday lives. Context includes environmental factors that make up the physical, social, and attitudinal environments within which people live and conduct their lives and personal factors that are characteristics of a person such as gender, age, race, motivation, and so forth.

Constitutive Definition of Intellectual Disability Defining a construct (e.g., intellectual disability) in relation to other constructs (such as an etiological, multidimensional model of human functioning and individualized supports).

Critical Thinking Skills Skills such as analysis, evaluation, interpretation, and inference that are involved in the synthesis of information.

Cutoff Score Score(s) that determines the boundaries of the "significant limitations in intellectual functioning and adaptive behavior criteria" for a diagnosis of intellectual disability. For both criteria, the cutoff score is approximately two standard deviations below the mean of the respective assessment instrument, considering the standard error of measurement for the specific instrument used and the strengths and limitations of the instrument.

Defining Explaining precisely the term, and establishing the term's meaning and boundaries.

Developmental Disability A severe, chronic, disability of an individual that (1) is attributable to a mental or physical impairment or a combination of mental and physical impairment; (2) is manifested before the individual attains age 22; (3) is likely to continue indefinitely; (4) results in substantial functional limitations in three or more of the following major life activities: self-care, receptive and expressive language, learning, mobility, self-direction, capacity for independent living, and economic self-sufficiency; and (5) reflects the individual's need for a combination and sequence of special, interdisciplinary, or generic service, individualized supports, or other forms of assistance that are lifelong or extended duration and are individually planned and coordinated (Developmental Disabilities Assistance and Bill of Rights Act of 2000 [Public Law 106–402; 102(8)(a)]).

Diagnosis The identification of intellectual disability based on three criteria: (1) significant limitations in intellectual functioning; (2) significant limitations in adaptive behavior as expressed in cognitive, social, and practical adaptive skills; and (3) age of onset prior to age 18.

Disability   The expression of limitations in individual functioning within a social context that represents a substantial disadvantage to the individual.

Ecological Model   A focus on person–environmental interaction and its impact on human functioning. Human functioning is facilitated by the congruence between personal competence and environmental demands and the provision of individualized supports.

Etiology   A branch of knowledge concerned with all of the causes of a particular phenomenon. In the 11th edition of the manual, etiology is presented as a multifactorial construct comprising four categories of risk factors (biomedical, social, behavioral, and educational) that interact across time and affect the individual's overall functioning.

Faking   Attempting to gain a benefit by deliberately attempting to look bad. See also **Malingering**

False negative   Person is actually an individual with intellectual disability but is incorrectly or falsely not diagnosed as such.

False positive   Person is incorrectly or falsely diagnosed as an individual with intellectual disability but actually is not.

Flynn Effect   The increase in IQ scores over time. The Flynn Effect raises potential challenges in the interpretation of IQ scores, with the recommendation that in cases in which a test with aging norms is used as part of a diagnosis of intellectual disability, a correction for the age of the norms is warranted.

Gullibility   This characteristic of many persons with intellectual disability includes occurrences of being successfully fooled, tricked, or lied to by others.

Health   A state of complete physical, mental, and social well-being.

Human Functioning   An umbrella term referring to all life activities of an individual and encompasses body structures and functions, personal activities, and participation. The 11th edition of the manual is based on a multidimensional model of human functioning that includes five dimensions (intellectual abilities, adaptive behavior, health, participation, and context) and the key role played by individualized supports.

Individuals with Intellectual Disability with Higher IQs   Persons with intellectual disability whose IQ score(s) is slightly *below* the ceiling of 70–75. This group shares much in common with individuals without a diagnosis of intellectual disability whose functioning is sometimes referred to as "borderline" (i.e., individuals who do not technically have intellectual disability but who have low IQs *above* the ceiling of approximately 70–75).

Informants   *See* **Respondents**

Intellectual Disability   A disability characterized by significant limitations in both intellectual functioning, and in adaptive behavior as expressed in conceptual, social, and practical adaptive skills. This disability originates before age 18. The following five assumptions are essential to the application of this definition: (1) limitations in present functioning must be considered within the context of community environments typical of the individual's age, peers, and culture; (2) valid assessment considers cultural and linguistic diversity as well as differences in communication, sensory, motor, and behavioral factors; (3) within an individual, limitations often coexist with strengths; (4) an important purpose of describing limitations is to develop a profile of needed supports; and (5) with appropriate personalized supports over a sustained period, the life functioning of the person with intellectual disability generally will improve.

Intellectual Disability Continuum Intellectual disability occurs along a continuum, as does intellectual ability, and should be described and understood in that way. AAIDD includes ALL individuals with intellectual disability who meet the criteria under one term: intellectual disability. It is not warranted to develop separate diagnoses or labels for individuals with higher IQs or for those with intellectual disability with lower IQs. By definition, all individuals with intellectual disability have significantly impaired intellectual functioning and adaptive behavior; whether at higher IQ or lower IQ, all individuals with intellectual disability fall within the definition.

Intellectual Functioning A broader term than either intellectual abilities or intelligence. The term reflects the fact that what is considered "intelligent behavior" is dependent on the other dimensions of human functioning: the adaptive behavior that one exhibits, the person's mental and physical health, the opportunities to participate in major life activities, and the context within which people live their everyday lives.

Intelligence A general mental capability. It includes reasoning, planning, solving problems, thinking abstractly, comprehending complex ideas, learning quickly, and learning from experience.

Maladaptive Behavior Behaviors that are challenging, difficult, or dangerous. Maladaptive behavior is not a characteristic or domain of adaptive behavior. Also referred to as "problem behavior" or "difficult behavior."

Malingering The intentional and purposeful feigning of an illness to achieve some recognizable goal or tangible benefit.

Measurement Error *See* **Standard Error of Measurement**

Mental Retardation An earlier term for intellectual disability. The term *intellectual disability* covers the same population of individuals who were diagnosed previously with mental retardation in number, kind, level, type, and duration of the disability and the need by people with this disability for individualized services and supports. Furthermore, every individual who is or was eligible for a diagnosis of mental retardation is eligible for a diagnosis of intellectual disability.

Multidimensional Classification System An approach to classification based on the five dimensions associated with human functioning (intellectual abilities, adaptive behavior, health, participation, and context) and the pattern and intensity of the individual's support needs.

Naiveté Overly trusting of others, immature, innocent, or inexperienced.

Naming Attaching a specific term (e.g., intellectual disability) to something or someone. Naming is a powerful process that carries many messages about perceived value and human relationships.

Operational Definition Defining a construct on the basis of how it is observed and measured. In reference to intellectual disability, three criteria are used to operationally define intellectual disability: significant limitations in intellectual functioning, adaptive behavior, and age of onset before age 18.

Outcomes Personal, family, or societal changes or benefits that follow as a result or consequence of some activity, intervention, or service.

Participation The performance of people in activities in social life domains.

Positive Behavior Supports An intervention strategy that involves (1) a functional assessment that defines the problem behavior, determines what maintains it, and describes the environmental context associated with high and low rates of behavior, and (2) a focus on two primary modes of intervention: altering the environment before a problem behavior occurs and teaching appropriate behaviors as a strategy for eliminating the need for problem behaviors to be exhibited.

Practical Skills Adaptive skills that include activities of daily living (personal care), occupational skills, use of money, safety, health care, travel or transportation, schedules or routines, and use of telephone.

Professional Ethics A set of principles that describe a system of moral behavior and a set of rules of conduct recognized in respect to a particular class of human actions or a particular group.

Professional Standards Authoritative criteria that provide the basis for professional activities such as evaluating professional practices, personnel preparation, accreditation, and quality control.

Quality Improvement An organization or system's capacity to improve performance and accountability through systematically collecting and analyzing data and information and implementing action strategies based on the analysis. Its goal is to improve human functioning and personal outcomes by enhancing policies, practices, training, technical assistance, and other individual, organization, or systems-level supports.

Quality Management Management strategies that focus on organizational performance and valued personal outcomes.

Reliability The measurement consistency of a test or assessment instrument.

Respondents Individuals who know the person well, who have observed the person across different community environments and situations, who have formally observed the person over time, and who provide information to a professional conducting an adaptive behavior interview.

Retrospective Diagnosis A diagnosis made later (i.e., after age 18) in a person's life and when the individual with intellectual disability did not receive the official diagnosis during the developmental period. For such a diagnosis, the clinician must use other sources of information, including possible obtainable data and the person's history to determine manifestation of possible intellectual disability prior to age 18. Important guidelines for determining a retrospective diagnosis are discussed in Chapter 3 of this guide.

Services   An organized means for delivering supports, instructions, therapies, or other forms of assistance.

Significant Limitations   See **Cutoff Score**

Social Judgment   Judgment based on interpersonal competence, problem-solving skills, and decision-making skills. Individuals with intellectual disability are frequently vulnerable to risks because of their lack of social judgment.

Social Skills   Adaptive skills that include interpersonal skills, social responsibility, self-esteem, avoiding gullibility, following rules and obeying laws, avoiding victimization, and social problem solving.

Standard Error of Measurement   The variation around a hypothetical "true score" for the person. The standard error of measurement applies only to scores obtained from a standardized test and can be estimated from the standard deviation of the test and a measure of the test's reliability. The standard error of measurement, which varies by test, subgroup, and age group, should be used to establish a statistical confidence interval within which the person's true score falls. For example, in reference to an IQ score of 70 (which corresponds to the "cutoff score" of approximately 2 SDs below the mean of the respective assessment instrument), the score of 70 is most accurately understood not as a precise score but as a range of confidence with parameters of at least one standard error of measurement (i.e., scores of about 66–74, 66% probability) or parameters of 2 SEM (i.e., scores of about 62–78, 95% probability). Reporting the range within which the person's true score falls, rather than only a score, underlies both the appropriate use of intellectual and adaptive behavior assessment instruments and best diagnostic practices in the field of intellectual disability. Such reporting must be a part of any decision concerning the diagnosis of intellectual disability.

Standard Deviation   An index of the amount of variability from the average (mean) score in a set of data. The standard deviation reflects the dispersion of scores in a distribution.

Standardized Measures   Measures of intellectual functioning, adaptive behavior, and support needs that have been developed on the basis of an underlying construct or theory and have demonstrated reliability, validity, and normative comparison groups. *See also* **Technical Adequacy**

Supports   Resources and strategies that aim to promote the development, education, interests, and personal well-being of a person and enhance individual functioning. Services are one type of support provided by professionals and agencies.

Support Needs   A psychological construct referring to the pattern and intensity of supports necessary for a person to participate in activities linked with normative human functioning.

Systems of Supports The planned and integrated use of individualized support strategies and resources such as organization systems, incentives, cognitive supports, tools, physical environment, skills and knowledge acquisition, and building on inherent ability. Systems of supports encompass the multiple aspects of human performance in multiple settings. A systems of supports model provides a structure for the organization and enhancement of human performance elements that are interdependent and cumulative.

Systems Perspective Integrating into one's thinking and actions the four systems that impact human functioning: (1) *microsystem* that includes the immediate social setting including the person, family, friends, colleagues, and close support staff; (2) *mesosystem* that includes the neighborhood, community, or organizations providing services or supports; (3) *macrosystem* that is the overarching patterns of culture, society, larger population, country, or sociopolitical influences; and (4) *chronosystem* that reflects the interactions of the person and multiple systems over time.

Technical Adequacy An essential requirement of assessment instruments. Criteria include content and construct validity, reliability, stability of measures, generalization of scores, predictive validity, and appropriateness to the individual or group being assessed.

Universal Design for Learning The design of instructional materials and activities that allow learning goals to be achievable by individuals with wide differences in abilities.

Validity The ability of the test or assessment instrument to measure what it was designed to measure.

REFERENCES

Ailey, S. H., & Hart, R. (2010). Hospital program for working with adult clients with intellectual and developmental disabilities. *Intellectual and Developmental Disabilities, 48,* 145–147.

American Psychiatric Association. (2000). *Diagnostic and statistical manual of mental disorders* (4th ed., text rev.). Washington, DC: Author.

Association of University Centers on Disabilities (AUCD). (2011). *Electronic toolkit of training resources for medical, dental, and nursing students.* Washington, DC: Author.

Bambara, L. M., Koger, F., & Bartholomew, A. (2011). Building skills for home and community. In M. E. Snell and F. Brown (Eds.), *Instruction of students with severe disabilities* (7th ed., pp. 529–568). Upper Saddle River, NJ: Merrill/Prentice-Hall.

Buntinx, W. H. E., & Schalock, R. (2010). Models of disability, quality of life, and individualized supports: Implications for professional practice in intellectual disability. *Journal of Policy and Practice in Intellectual Disabilities, 7*(4), 283–294.

Carter, E. W., Hughes, C., Guth, C., & Copeland, S. R. (2005). Factors influencing social interaction among high school students with intellectual disabilities and their general education peers. *American Journal on Mental Retardation, 110,* 366–377.

Carter, E. W., & Kennedy, C. H. (2006). Promoting access to the general curriculum using peer support strategies. *Research and Practice for Persons with Severe Disabilities, 31,* 1–9.

Carter, E. W., Sisco, L. G., Melekoglu, M. A., & Kurkowski, C. (2007). Peer supports as an alternative to individually assigned paraprofessionals in inclusive high school classrooms. *Research and Practice for Persons with Severe Disabilities, 32,* 213–227.

Center for Child and Human Development. (2009). *Transition of care guide: A guide for community support providers to facilitate safe transitions from the hospital or long term care facility to home.* Washington, DC: Georgetown University Press.

Council on Quality and Leadership. (2005). *Personal outcome measures.* Towson, MD: Author.

Dean, A. C., Victor, T. L., Boone, K. B., & Arnold, G. (2008). The relationship of IQ to effort test performance. *Clinical Neuropsychologist, 22,* 705–722.

Doane, B. M., & Salekin, K. L. (2008). Susceptibility of current adaptive behavior measures to feigned deficits. *Law and Human Behavior.* DOI 10, 1007/s10979-008-9157-5.

Doyle, M. B. (2008). *The paraprofessional's guide to the inclusive classroom: Working as a team* (3rd ed.). Baltimore: Paul H. Brookes.

Dunst, C. J., Trivette, C. M., & Snyder, D. (2000). Family-professional partnerships: A behavioral science perspective. In M. Fine and L. Sherrod (Eds.). *Collaboration with parents and families of children and youth with exceptionalities* (2nd ed., pp. 27–48). Austin, TX: PRO-ED.

References

Edgerton, R. (1967). *The cloak of competence: Stigma in the lives of the mentally retarded.* Berkeley: University of California Press.

Emerson, E., Robertson, J., Hatton, C., Knapp, M., Walsh, P., & Hallam, A. (2005). Costs and outcomes of community residential supports in England. In R. Stancliffe and K. Lakin (Eds.). *Costs and outcomes of community services for people with intellectual disabilities* (pp. 151–174). Baltimore: Paul H. Brookes.

Ferguson, D. L. (2008). International trends in inclusive education: The continuing challenge to teach each one and everyone. *European Journal of Special Needs Education, 23,* 109–120.

Finlay, W. M., & Lyons, E. (2002). Acquiescence in interviews with people who have mental retardation. *Mental Retardation, 40,* 14–29.

Fletcher, J. M., Stuebing, K. K., & Hughes, L. C. (2010). IQ scores should be corrected for the Flynn effect in high-stakes decisions. *Journal of Psychoeducational Assessment, 28,* 469–473.

Flynn, J. R. (2006). Tethering the elephant: Capital cases, IQ, and the Flynn Effect. *Psychology, Public Policy, and Law, 12,* 170–198.

Fuchs, D., & Deshler, D. D. (2007). What we need to know about responsiveness to intervention (and shouldn't be afraid to ask). *Learning Disabilities Research & Practice, 22,* 129–136.

Giangreco, M. F., Edelman, S., Luiselli, T. E., & MacFarland, S. (1997). Helping or hovering? Effects of instructional assistant proximity on students with disabilities. *Exceptional Children, 64,* 7–18.

Greenspan, S. (2006). Functional concepts in mental retardation: Finding the natural essence of an artificial category. *Exceptionality, 14,* 205–224.

Greenspan, S. (2011). Intellectually disabled homicide defendants: Issues in diagnosing intellectual disability in capital cases. *Exceptionality, 19*(4), 1–19.

Greenspan, S., & Switzky, H. N. (2006). Lessons learned from the Atkins decision in the next AAMR manual. In H. N. Switzky and S. Greenspan (Eds.), *What is mental retardation? Ideas for an evolving disability in the 21st Century* (pp. 283–302). Washington, DC: American Association on Mental Retardation.

Gresham, F. M., & Reschly, D. J. (2011). Standards of practice and Flynn Effect testimony in death penalty cases. *Intellectual and Developmental Disabilities, 49*(3), 131–140.

Hayes, J. S., Hale, D. B., & Gouvier, W. D. (1997). Do tests predict malingering in defendants with mental retardation? *Journal of Psychology, 131,* 575–576.

Horner, R. H., Sugai, G., & Anderson, C. M. (2010). Examining the evidence base for school-wide positive behavior support. *Focus on Exceptional Children, 42*(8), 1–14.

Hurley, K. E., & Deal, W. P. (2006). Assessment instruments measuring malingering used with individuals who have mental retardation: Potential problems and issues. *Mental Retardation, 44,* 112–119.

Institute of Medicine (2007). *The future of disability in America.* Washington, DC: National Academics Press.

Jacobson, J. W., & Mulick, J. A. (2006). Ten years later: Two AAMR tales of a condition. In H. N. Switzky and S. Greenspan (Eds.), *What is mental retardation: Ideas for an evolving disability in the 21st Century* (pp. 187–196). Washington, DC: American Association on Mental Retardation.

Janney, R. E., & Snell, M. E., (2004). *Practices for inclusive schools: Modifying schoolwork* (2nd ed.). Baltimore: Paul H. Brookes.

Janney, R. E., & Snell, M. E. (2011). Designing and implementing instruction for inclusive classes. In M. E. Snell and F. Brown (Eds.), *Instruction of students with severe disabilities* (pp. 453–492). Upper Saddle River, NJ: Merrill/Prentice-Hall.

Kaufman, A. S. (1994). Practice effects. In R. J. Sternbery (Ed.), *Encyclopedia of human intelligence* (Vol. 2, pp. 828–833). New York: MacMillan.

Kaufman, A. S. (2010). Looking through Flynn's rose-colored scientific spectacles. *Journal of Psychoeducational Assessment, 28,* 494–505.

Keith, K. D., & Bonham, G. S. (2005). The use of quality of life data at the organization and systems level. *Journal of Intellectual Disability Research, 49,* 799–805.

Keyes, D. W. (2004). Use of the Minnesota Multiphasic Personality Inventory (MMPI) to identify malingering in mental retardation. *Mental Retardation, 42,* 151–154.

Krahn, G. L., Fujiura, G., Drum, C. E., Cardinal, B. J., Nosek, M. A., et al. (2009). The dilemma of measuring perceived health status in the context of disability. *Disability and Health Journal, 2,* 49–56.

Larson, S. A., Lakin, K. C., Anderson, L., Lee, N. K., Lee, J. H., & Anderson, D. (2001). Prevalence of mental retardation and developmental disabilities: Estimates from the 1994/1995 National Health Interview Survey Disability Supplements. *American Journal on Mental Retardation, 106,* 231–252.

Luckasson, R., Borthwick-Duffy, S., Buntinx, W. H. E., Coulter, D. L., Craig, E. M., Reeve, A., et al. (2002). *Mental retardation: Definition, classification, and systems of supports* (10th ed.). Washington, DC: American Association on Mental Retardation.

Luckasson, R., Coulter, D. L., Polloway, E. A., Reiss, S., Schalock, R. L., Snell, M. E., et al. (1992). Mental retardation: Definition, classification, and systems of supports (9th ed.). Washington, DC: American Association on Mental Retardation.

Lukens, J., & Hurrell, M. (1996). A comparison of the Stanford Binet IV and the WISC-III with mildly retarded children. *Psychology in the Schools, 33,* 24–27.

MacVaugh, G. S., & Cunningham, M. D. (2009). Atkins vs. Virginia: Implications and recommendations for forensic practice. *Journal of Psychiatry and Law, 37,* 131–187.

MEDSTAT Group, Inc. (2003). *The Participant Experience Survey: MR/DD Version.* Baltimore, MD: Centers for Medicare and Medicaid Services.

References

National Association of County and City Health Officials. (2011). Tips and strategies for successful integration of people with disabilities into local public health promotion programs. [Fact sheet]. Washington, DC: Author.

National Core Indicators. (2003). *National core indicators: 5 years of performance measurement.* Alexandria, VA: National Association on State Directors of Developmental Disabilities Services (NASDDDS) and Human Services Research Institute.

Nelson, W., & Dacey, C. (1999). Validity of the Stanford-Binet Intelligence Scale-IV: Its use in young adults with mental retardation. *Mental Retardation, 37,* 319–325.

Newman, L., Wagner, M., Cameto, R., & Knokey, A. M. (2009). *The post-high school outcomes of youth with disabilities up to 4 years after high school. A report of findings from the National Longitudinal Transition Study-2 (NLTS2) (NCSER 2009–3017).* Menlo Park, CA: SRI International.

Newman, L., Wagner, M., Cameto, R., Knokey, A. M., & Shaver, D. (2010). *Comparisons across time of the outcomes of youth with disabilities up to 4 years after high school. A report of findings from the National Longitudinal Transition Study-2 (NLTS2).* Menlo Park, CA: SRI International.

Olmstead v. L. C., 527 U.S. 581 (1999).

Papay, C. K., & Bambara, L. M. (2011). Postsecondary education for transition-age students with intellectual and other developmental disabilities: A national survey. *Education and Training in Autism and Developmental Disabilities, 46,* 78–93.

Perry, J., & Felce, D. (2005). Factors associated with outcomes in community group homes. *American Journal on Mental Retardation, 110*(2), 121–135.

Reynolds, C. R., Niland, J., Wright, J. E., & Rosenn, M. (2010). Failure to apply the Flynn correction in death penalty litigation: Standards of practice of today maybe, but certainly malpractice of tomorrow. *Journal of Psychoeducational Assessment, 28,* 477–481.

Rose, D. H., & Meyer, A. (2002). *Teaching every student in the Digital Age: Universal design for learning.* Alexandria, VA: Association for Supervision and Curriculum Development (ASCD).

Rush University Medical Center (2011). *Programs related to disability rights and accommodations.* Retrieved September 7, 2011, from http://www.ruishu.rush.edu/servlet

Schalock, R. L., Borthwick-Duffy, S. A., Bradley, V. J., Buntinx, W. H. E., Coulter, D. L., Craig, E. M., et al. (2010). *Intellectual disability: Definition, classification, and systems of supports.* Washington, DC : American Association on Intellectual and Developmental Disabilities.

Schalock, R. L., & Luckasson, R. (2005). *Clinical judgment.* Washington, DC: American Association on Mental Retardation.

Shogren, K. A., & Turnbull, H. R. (2010). Public policy and outcomes for persons with intellectual disability: Extending and expanding the public policy framework of the 11th edition of Intellectual disability: Definition, classification, and systems of supports. *Intellectual and Developmental Disabilities, 48,* 387–392.

Silverman, W., Miezejeski, C., Ryan, R., Zigman, W., Krinsky-McHale, S., & Urv, T. (2010). Stanford-Binet and WAIS IQ differences and their implications for adults with intellectual disability (a.k.a. mental retardation). *Intelligence, 38*, 242–248.

Sloan, M., & Irvin C. (2007). *Money follows the person Quality of Life Survey. Prepared for CMS.* Washington, DC: Mathematica Policy Research, Inc.

Snell, M. A., & Luckasson, R. A., with Borthwick-Duffy, S., Bradley, V. J., Buntinx, W. H. E., Coulter, D. L., et al. (2009). The characteristics and needs of people with intellectual disability who have higher IQ scores. *Intellectual and Developmental Disabilities, 47*(3), 220–233.

Stancliffe, R., & Lakin, C. (Eds.). (2005). *Costs and outcomes of community services for people with intellectual disabilities.* Baltimore: Paul H. Brookes.

Tasse, M. J., Schalock, R. L., Balboni, G., Bersani, H., Borthwick-Duffy, S. A., Spreat, S. et al. (in press). The construct of adaptive behavior: Its conceptualization, measurement, and use in the field of intellectual disability. *Intellectual and Developmental Disabilities.*

Test, D. W., & Massotti, V. L. (2011). Transitioning from school to employment. In M. E. Snell and F. Brown (Eds.), *Instruction of students with severe disabilities* (7th ed., pp. 569–611). Upper Saddle River, NJ: Merrill/Prentice-Hall.

Thoma, C. A., & Wehman, P. (2010). *Getting the most out of IEPs: An educators guide to the student-directed approach.* Baltimore: Paul H. Brookes.

Thompson, J. R., Bradley, V., Buntinx, W. H. E., Schalock, R. L., Shogren, K. A., Snell, M., & Wehmeyer, M. L. (2009). Conceptualizing supports and the support needs of people with intellectual disability. *Intellectual and Developmental Disabilities, 47*(2), 135–146.

Thompson, J. R., Bryant, B. R., Campbell, E. M., Craig, E. M., Hughes, C. M., et al. (2004). *Supports Intensity Scale. Users' manual.* Washington, DC: American Association on Mental Retardation.

Turnbull, A., Turnbull, H. R., Erwin, E. J., Soodak, L. C., & Shogren, K. A. (2010). *Families, professionals, and exceptionality: Positive outcomes through partnerships and trust* (6th ed.). Upper Saddle River, NJ: Merrill/Prentice-Hall.

Turnbull, H. R., Beegle, G., & Stowe, M. J. (2001a). The core concepts of disability policy affecting families who have children with disabilities. *Journal of Disability Policy Studies, 12*(3), 133–143.

Turnbull, H. R., & Stowe, M. J. (2001). A taxonomy for organizing the core concepts according to their underlying principles. *Journal of Disability Policy Studies, 12*(3), 177–197.

Turnbull, H. R., Wilcox, B. L., Stowe, M. J., & Umbarger, G. T. (2001b). Matrix of federal statutes and federal and state court decisions reflecting the core concepts of disability policy. *Journal of Disability Policy Studies, 12*(3), 144–176.

U.S. Department of Education, Office of Special Education and Rehabilitative Services, Office of Special Education Programs. (2010). *29th Annual Report to Congress on the*

References

Implementation of the Individuals with Disabilities Education Act, 2007, vol. 2. Washington, DC: Government Printing Office.

U.S. Department of Health and Human Services. (2005). *The Surgeon General's call to action to improve the health and wellness of persons with disabilities.* Washington, DC: Government Printing Office.

United Nations (2006). *Convention on the rights of persons with disabilities.* Retrieved April 15, 2011, from http://www.un.org/disabilities

United Nations Educational, Scientific and Cultural Organization (UNESCO). (2009). *Inclusive education: The way of the future.* Geneva: UNESCO. Available at http://www.ibe.unesco.org/en/ice/48th-ice-2008/final-report.html

Verdugo, M. A., & Rodríguez, A. (2012). La inclusión educativa en España desde la perspectiva de alumnos con discapacidad intelectual, familias y profesionales. *Revista de Educación, 358.* DOI: 10-4438/1988-592X-RE-2010-358-086.

Verdugo, M. A., Schalock, R. L., Navas, P., & Gomez, L. E. (in press). The concept of quality of life and its role in enhancing human rights in the field of intellectual disability. *Journal of Intellectual Disability Research.*

World Health Organization (WHO). (2001). *International classification of functioning, disability, and health* (ICF). Geneva: Author.

Zeithaml, V. A., Bitner, M. J., & Gremler, D. D. (2006). *Services marketing: Integrating customer focus across the firm.* New York, NY: McGraw-Hill.

SUBJECT INDEX

AAIDD Public Policy Framework
   Implications   54–57
   See also Public policy, Policy outcomes
AAIDD System
   Relation to families and advocates   59–62
   Relation to other systems   5
   Relevance to professionalism and professional responsibilities   7–11
Adaptive behavior
   Assessment of   19
   Definition   69
   Framework   17–18
   Self ratings   22
   Significant limitations   17–18
Advocates and advocacy   61–62
   Assessment Framework   2–3, 61
Best practices   7–8
Context
Clinical judgment
   Characteristics   4–5, 9
   Definition   4–5
   Purpose   4
   See also Clinical judgment strategies
Clinical judgment strategies   16–22
Conceptual skills   17
Confidence interval   24
Cutoff score   24–25
Diagnosis
   Complex diagnostic situations: See Clinical strategies
   Criteria for a diagnosis of intellectual disability   1, 63–64
Disability core concepts   50
Educating students with ID
   Accessing the general education culture   30
   Accommodations   29–30
   Collaborative planning   35–36
   Curriculum adaptations   31–34
   Education supports   30–35
   Instructional adaptations   34–35
   Team roles and responsibilities   36
   Transition   36–39
Etiology
   Multifactorial approach   3–4, 66–67
Faking   25
   See also Malingering
False negative   21
False positive   21
Family members   59
   See also Parents
Flynn Effect   25
Forensic issues   20–22
   Guidelines when dealing with   26–27
Fostering justice   26–27
   Foundational aspects of ID in fostering justice   26–27
   Guidelines for fostering justice   22–27
Health
   Definition   64
   Implications of 11th Edition for health care professionals   63–67
Holistic approach   66–67
Human functioning
   Conceptual framework   3, 64
   ID as a part of human functioning   59–60
   Multidimensionality   1–2, 59–61, 64
Intellectual disability
   Assumptions essential to applying the definition   1
   Characteristics of persons with ID with higher IQ scores   16
   Definition   1, 63–64
   Foundational aspects   26–27
   Multidimensionality of   1–2
   Strength-based approach   60
Intelligence
   Assessment of   19
   Definition   2
Malingering   26
   See also Faking

Organizations providing supports
    Focusing their supports   42–43
    Quality management   43–47
    Understanding their role   41–42
Parents
    Input and support within education settings/processes   36
Personal outcomes   43
    Quality of life domains   45, 52
Policy outcomes
    Family outcomes   51–52, 54
    Personal outcomes   51
    Societal outcomes   53
    Systems change indicators   53
Practical skills   18
Practice effect   25
Professional ethics   9
Professional responsibilities
    In assessment of intellectual functioning   9–10
    In assessment of adaptive behavior   10
    In classification   11
    In planning supports   11
Professional standards   8
Professionalism   7–8
    Best practices   7–8, 55
Public policy
    Administration principles   50–51
    Core disability concepts   50
    Constitutional principles   50
    Ethical principles   50
    See also AAIDD framework; Policy outcomes
Retrospective diagnosis   23–24
Social skills   17
Stereotypes   27–28
Subjective well-being   67
Support needs   42–43
Supports
    Behavioral   65
    Communication   65
    Continuity of care   65
    Educational   30–35
    Framework   4
Systems of supports   43–44
Supports planning   4
Synthesizing obtained information   21–22
UN *Convention on the Rights of Persons with Disabilities*
    Articles   43
    Relationship between Articles and quality of life domains   45